齊物
逍遙
2020
—
2021

黃效文——著

ENLIGHTENED
SOJOURN

Authored and Photographed by Wong How Man

Wong How Man

Time Magazine honored Wong How Man among their 25 Asian Heroes in 2002, calling Wong "China's most accomplished living explorer". CNN has featured his work over a dozen times, including a half-hour profile by anchor Richard Quest. Discovery Channel has made several documentaries about his work. The Wall Street Journal has also featured him on its front page.

Wong began exploring China in 1974. He is Founder/President of the China Exploration & Research Society, a non-profit organization specializing in exploration, research, conservation and education in remote China and neighboring countries. Wong has led six major expeditions for the National Geographic. He successfully defined the sources of the Yangtze, Mekong, Yellow River, Salween, Irrawaddy and the Brahmaputra rivers.

His organization conducts nature and culture conservation projects covering China and neighboring countries, including India, Nepal, Bhutan, Laos, Myanmar, the Philippines, and also Taiwan. Wong has authored over thirty books and has received many accolades, among them an honorary doctorate from his alma mater, the University of Wisconsin at River Falls, and the Lifetime Achievement Award from Monk Hsing Yun of Taiwan. He has been keynote speaker at many international functions.

黃
效
文

《時代雜誌》曾選黃效文為亞洲二十五位英雄之一，稱他為「中國最有成就的在世探險家」。*CNN* 報導過黃效文的各項工作超過十二次之多，其中還包括主播 *Richard Quest* 的三十分鐘專訪。探索頻道也為他做的工作製作了好幾個紀錄片。《華爾街日報》也曾用頭版報導過他。

黃效文自一九七四年開始在中國探險。他是中國探險學會的創辦人和會長，這是個非營利組織，致力於在中國偏遠地區及鄰近國家的探險，研究，保育和教育工作。他曾經在美國《國家地理雜誌》帶領過六個重要的探險。他成功地定位的源頭包括長江，湄公河，黃河，薩爾溫江，伊洛瓦底江及雅魯藏布江。

他的學會主導的文化和自然保育項目橫跨中國和鄰近的國家，包括印度、尼泊爾、不丹、寮國、緬甸、菲律賓還有台灣。

黃效文著作的書超過三十本並獲得過許多榮譽，他的母校威斯康辛大學頒發給他名譽博士學位，星雲大師也贈與他「華人世界終身成就獎」。他也是許多國際會議裡的專題演講人。

Memories of Lhasa in 1946

When I was 16 years old, my mother Mayum Choni Wangmo Dorji took my sister Tashi and me to visit our 14-year-old brother, Ugyen, who had been recognized as the 8th incarnation of Chushul Boudhey Gomchen Pemaling Tulku.

My brother's religious name was Jetsun Jampal Ngawang Lodro Chokyi Gyaltshen.

During our stay in Lhasa, we visited the beautiful large monastery of Boudhey Gomchen Gompa in Chushul. It was famous for its ascetics who used to come from all over Tibet to meditate there.

The founding Lama was born in Bumthang and was believed to be either a descendant of the famous Bhutan Saint Terton Pema Lingpa or the Saint's disciple.

My mother, Tashi and I drove by car to Gangtok in Sikkim from where we rode on mules for 17 days to reach Lhasa.

In Lhasa, my mother stayed with her cousin Lhading Trungyig Chenmo, and my brother. While Tashi and I stayed in the lovely Taring House with my mother's brother Taring Raja's eldest son Kugno Jigme Taring and Mary Taring.

While in Lhasa, we met many holy lamas and enjoyed visiting the sacred Jokhang and Drepung, Sera and Ganden Monasteries.

We visited the magnificent Potala Palace and the rooms of His Holiness the Great 13th Dalai Lama Ngawang Lobzang Thubten Gyatso, who had been the Root Guru of my grandfather

1

Gongzim Raja Ugyen Dorji and his sister Ane Thubten Wangmo. He had stayed eight and a half months most happily in Bhutan House in Kalimpong.

We also visited the beautiful Norbu Lingka Palace and received an audience with the then 11-year-old, His Holiness the 14th Dalai Lama. His Holiness's mother, Gyalyum Chenmo was very kind to us and gave us tea.

We attended a grand party given by Kapsopa Shape in white tents pitched by the river Tsangpo, with elaborate banquets accompanied by traditional dances, singing and music.

Lhasa was a most sacred, beautiful and happy place with all the Tibetan people deeply religious and contented.

We feel so fortunate to have received the blessings of many great holy lamas, visited beautiful sacred sites like the Majestic Potala Palace, Norbulingka Palace, Chakpori, Drak Yerpa, Boudhey Gomchen Labrang and the exquisite Lukhang Temple at the base of the Potala Palace and seen Tibet filled with the blessings of Guru Rinpoche and the great Chogyals.

Kesang Choeden Wangchuck

Gyalyum Kesang Choeden Wangchuck
Her Majesty Royal Grand Queen Mother of Bhutan.

2

十六歲那年，我的母親馬攸姆瓊英旺姆多吉 (Mayum Choni Wangmo Dorji)，帶著姐姐扎西 (Tashi) 和我，前往西藏探望我們十四歲的弟弟烏顏 (Ugyen)，他當時被認證為第八世楚舒勒貢倩白瑪林祖古轉世活佛 (Chushul Boudhey Gomchen Pemaling Tulku)。

我弟弟的宗教法名為：吉增強巴阿旺羅哲碓吉嘉參 (Jetsun Jampal Ngawang Lodro Chokyi Gyaltshen)。

在拉薩逗留那段期間，我們參觀了曲水縣的莊嚴大廟，降曲林寺。這是一座以戒律聞名的寺廟，吸引西藏各地苦修者前來靜修冥想。

創廟的喇嘛，出生於不丹布姆唐 (Bumthang)，一般相信這位喇嘛可能是不丹著名伏藏大師貝瑪林巴 (Terton Pema Lingpa) 聖賢的後代或弟子。

我的母親，姐姐扎西和我，驅車出發，抵達錫金的甘托克 (Gangtok) 後，再由此騎騾十七天，才輾轉抵達拉薩。

到拉薩後，我的母親帶著弟弟住在親戚拉吞友乾姆 (Lhading Trungyig Chenmo) 的家。而扎西和我則到溫馨的次仁之家，與我舅舅拉加次仁的長子夫婦根諾晋美次仁 (Kugno Jigme Taring) 與瑪莉次仁，同住數日。

遊歷拉薩期間，我們有幸與多位喇嘛見面，也參訪不少聖殿廟宇，包括大昭寺、哲蚌寺、色拉寺與甘丹寺等。

此外，我們也參觀了壯麗的布達拉宮，與藏傳佛教格魯派第十三世達賴喇嘛土登嘉措的起居室。這位西藏最高領袖，曾是我祖父拉加烏顏多吉 (Gongzim Raja Ugyen Dorji) 與姑婆土登旺姆 (Ane Thubten Wangmo) 靈性啟蒙的尊貴上師。他曾在噶倫堡 (Kalimpong) 的不丹之家，度過最悠然快樂的八個半月。

我們到典雅的羅布林卡皇宮，並在那裡與當時才十一歲的第十四世達賴喇嘛見面，至

尊達賴的母親，聖母德吉次仁待人親切和善，特別奉茶來接待我們。

此外，我們還參加了一場盛大的派對饗宴，地點就在雅魯藏布江旁的白色帳篷內，除了豐盛與精緻美食外，還有傳統歌舞與音樂表演，門庭赫奕，熱鬧非凡。

因藏族對信仰的潛心追求與知足感恩之心，而使拉薩自成一個神聖、迷人、自得其樂的地方。

我此生能接受眾多至尊喇嘛的加持，還有機會親臨氣勢恢宏的布達拉宮、羅布林卡皇宮、藥王山、扎耶巴寺、降曲林寺，以及位於布達拉宮基地一座精美雅緻的魯康寺，同時親眼見證西藏這塊土地如何領受多位仁波切導師與大寶法王的祝福，我為此而深感榮幸。

格桑曲登旺曲 *Gyalyum Kesang Choeden Wangchuck*
不丹皇室皇太后

Preface
"Enlightened Sojourn" 2020-2021

I owe it to my readers to provide a short introduction to the Preface written by the Royal Grandmother of Bhutan in the preceding pages. We became close friends through my trips and projects in her beloved kingdom, and we have corresponded frequently. While in Lhasa, I took an evening photograph of the Potala Palace and sent it as a birthday wish for her 91st birthday.

That triggered old memories of her own visit to the sacred city in 1946 as a young princess of 16 , seventy-five years ago. Thus it was that I asked her to write a Preface for this book, revisiting her trip to Lhasa. She gracefully accepted, and what she has written will become an important record of the changes in the intervening years, across three quarters of a century. It serves not only as a Preface to this book, but as an archival document recording things never before published.

As for my own writing, the pandemic has been both a curse and a blessing.

As a curse, I was not able to leave home for a year and could not go into the field, which I love so much. As a blessing, I ended up writing Home Reports rather than Field Reports, allowing myself to delve into our library of fine books for research and provide greater detail in my writing.

While field reports bring a certain ingenuity and definitely come with more emotions attached, home reports provide reference and more in-depth perception. One requires more right-brain activities, the other more left-brain analysis. They are, however, not mutually exclusive.

And, as I explored closer to home, we quickly started multiple projects within the confines of Hong Kong and managed to produce some early results.

I am used to going to places into which few others can penetrate and to implementing projects in some of the most remote regions using our fleet of off-road cars and even our own exploration boats. Now, I take the ferry and bus to get to our project sites a couple of hours of traveling time away from my home. It is, as the Chinese saying goes, "killing a chicken using an ox knife," pertaining to underuse of one's skill set.

A few months into the projects, just as we gained traction and the first results were showing, I almost abandoned ship, as I found the gratification and satisfaction was small as compared to when I worked far afield. Within a couple of weeks, however, I self-corrected my thought and found a new impetus to continue the work we had started near home. I realized that the new generation of youngsters that I often get in touch with is from an internet age, with less patience and of course, due to age, far less experience and resources. They often look for instant gratification, as well as being easily distracted.

That is an opportunity for our near-home projects. These projects are small and with fast return.

They should be ideal as case studies for the younger set, demonstrating that, with less capacity and support, they too can start something worthy within their community or vicinity. Furthermore, a conservation project is usually done only once, but as a teaching model and case study, it can have a very long lifespan.

Thus, parts of this new book, among other articles, reflect some of our latest explorations and projects, all within close range to my home in Hong Kong. Like wars and diseases throughout the ages, this pandemic will subside and be controlled in time. And when the sky, ocean and borders open again, my team and I will once again explore beyond the distant horizon, where the sky, land and sea merge into one.

Indeed, in early 2021, after three weeks of quarantine in Macau, I once again embarked on a field trip in China. It lasted almost four months, about which I shall share with my friends in the near future.

Wong How Man
Founder/President CERS

前言

託讀者之福，獲不丹皇室皇太后為本書前頁提筆撰寫序言，深感榮幸，也為此寫一段簡介。我多番前往不丹進行一些項目，因此與皇太后成為好友，經常互通音訊。當我在拉薩時，特別拍了一張夕陽映照下的布達拉宮影像，寄給太后慶賀她九十一歲生日。

那張照片牽動她的往日記憶——帶她回到一九四六年，七十五年前當她還是十六歲的公主時，曾親臨拉薩這座聖城。我藉此機會請她為本書寫序，同時邀請她重訪拉薩。她欣然允諾，而她所寫的這段文字，將成為這些年間世局變動下的重要記錄，那是跨越四分之三世紀的滄海與桑田。事實上，這不僅是本書推薦序，更是未曾發表過的文獻記錄，彌足珍貴。

對我個人的文字書寫而言，這波全球疫情之災，可謂禍福相倚。

這一年我都出不了遠門，無法上山下海，到各地查勘，此生最愛彷彿被剝奪了——此

乃禍。但應運而生的祝福是，我雖寫不成《田野報告》，但終於完成了《在家報告》；並在寫作過程中，發掘我們圖書館的不少典藏好書，深入鑽研，同時為讀者提供更詳實的細節。

如果說，《田野報告》充滿一手資料原創性與臨場帶來的種種感受，那麼，《在家報告》則提供更多元的參考方向與深度觀點。前者要求多一點右腦活動，後者則側重左腦分析。其實，兩者兼容並蓄，相輔相成。

當我在家附近進出探究時，即便外在環境將我們局限於香港之內，我們仍很快便啟動好幾項計劃與活動，在短時間內也收穫不少初步成果。

我向來喜歡到少人出入之地勘探尋索，藉由我們的越野車隊，甚至我們自己的探險船隻，跋山涉水，在最荒僻偏遠之處，籌備與展開一些項目。而今，受困城市的我，出門靠渡輪與公車，從家裡到計劃執行點，區區數小時便「一蹴可幾」。所謂「殺雞焉用牛刀」，感覺有些懷才不遇的悵然若失。

投入這些計劃方案幾個月後，雖然我們受歡迎的程度逐漸增強，初期成果也鼓舞人心，但我卻像隻擱淺野渡之棄舟，幾近心灰意冷，因為相對於「遠方與天涯」，我當下的滿足感與成就感是如此微弱。短短數週內，我慢慢調整與矯正我的想法，同時也找到新動力，來延續我在住家附近啟動的工作。我知道我所接觸的年輕族群，來自網路世代，他們耐心不足，加上年紀尚輕，更缺經驗與資源。他們亟欲尋求立即的肯定與滿足感，同時也容易分心走神。

我們在離家不遠處展開新計劃。這些主題小而美，立竿見影；看來是這群年輕人的理想個案研究，執行過程中或許產能與支援都稍顯捉襟見肘，但這番行動證明了他們也能在自己的社區鄰里，有一番作為與貢獻。更何況，保育計劃通常是一次性工作，但若以它作為教育模式與個案研究而言，社區型計劃反倒比較細水長流，影響深遠而長久。

因此，在眾多文章中，本書其中一部分內容特別呈現一些我們近期的探索行動，這些

計劃的執行地點都在香港之內，住家附近。一如每個世代曾歷經的戰役與疾病，這場全球疫情也將逐漸趨緩，及時受控。有一天，當海陸空邊界再度對外開放時，我與我的團隊將整裝待發，遠赴地角天涯——在地平線以外，海陸天相連之境。

其實，我已於二零二一年初時，在澳門熬過三週隔離期後，再度動身前往中國內地，踏上我的田野探索之旅。這趟遠行歷時四個月左右，其中過程與故事，我會在將來的文章中與我的朋友們分享。

黃效文

中國探險學會創辦人／會長

目次

島嶼尋訪

ISLAND PURSUIT

Kee Lung, Taiwan – November 24, 2019

ISLAND PURSUIT
Anxiety unfulfilled

I stand close to the boat's chimney on the aft deck. It is warming to both body and heart, evoking a nostalgic feeling buried deep inside, which I have totally forgotten for over half a century.

I am on a large ferry boat, the Taima Star (Tai for Taiwan and Ma for Matsu), with vehicles underdeck, out of Keelung, the northernmost port in Taiwan. It is late in the evening near midnight when we sail out toward the open sea. The four-year-old boat is 5000 tons with a length of over 100 meters. But my heart goes back to another Star, the Star Ferry in Hong Kong, barely 160 tons and one-third the length. Suddenly my teenage years come back to mind.

For six years, from 1961 to 1967 when I was twelve to eighteen years of age, I sat many times close to a chimney on the under deck of the ferry boat in Hong Kong during the winter months, riding across the harbor to Tsim Sha Tsui in Kowloon where I attended high school. Occasionally I would bring my ten-speed BSA bicycle along, an eye-catching luxury in Hong Kong during the 60s. In that case however, I would have to take the rival and less posh Yaumati Ferry from Wan Chai to Jordan Road, as the Star Ferry catered to a classier set and did not allow cargo, let alone a bicycle.

The exhaust flowing through the chimney provided heat from the engine room below. The lower deck had no windows to shield passengers from the cold northerly wind, and the wind was made more penetrating, as my young body was thin in those days. Those were the days before down jackets became affordable and popular, and a school uniform could barely provide enough warmth.

Upper deck charged HK twenty cents and lower deck half that. A proposal for a price hike precipitated a major riot in 1966, a year before my School Certificate Examination. The cheaper fare and lower deck came with a much-welcomed amenity for us kids - peddlers selling eateries in baskets they carried onto the boat. Upper deck was filled with gentlemen in suit and tie, whereas ladies would be in modern western dress or elegant "cheong-sam", the soon-to-be-eclipsed traditional Chinese dress.

My family lived on Tai Hang Road, mid-level Hong Kong above Causeway Bay. My school, a Jesuit high school, was on the Kowloon side on the peninsula across Victoria Harbor, thus the ferry boat ride each day, five days a week during summer and six days during winter. My boat ride and bike ride during those days quenched my earliest thirst for exploration.

Now I pace the deck of the Taima Star and sit at times on the picnic tables.

Star Ferry / 天星小輪
HM's home growing up / HM 成長的家鄉

This is my third attempt to reach Dongyin Island off the northern coast of Taiwan. Both times before my attempt to reach Dongyin were futile due first to a change in the boat schedule and later to an approaching typhoon.

Dongyin includes three small islands connected by dike-like bridges. The island is barely 4.5 square kilometer, about twice the size of the fishing island of Cheung Chau in Hong Kong. It is considered the northernmost point of Taiwan. The islands were once a heavily fortified citadel that the army of Taiwan held as highly strategic in defense of the main island from the threat of the People's Republic. Cruise missiles were said to be deployed there, though at the time of my visit I only saw from a distance old style anti-aircraft guns.

On May 1, 1965 some fifty-five years ago, a sea battle erupted off Dongyin between the Nationalists in Taiwan and the Navy of the PRC. During the beginning of the Cultural Revolution, the Mainland Chinese media gave little coverage of this skirmish, which involved only one Taiwanese destroyer and several Mainland gunboats. Had it been given more media attention, it would nonetheless be considered communist propaganda, given the style of reporting in China during those days. However, on the Taiwan side, it became a big news event and was quickly picked up by other western media, naturally.

At the time, the destroyer "Dongjiang" (East River) had just finished a major refurbishment and was being deployed north to guard the uppermost Dongyin Island. After the battle, the Nationalists subsequently admitted malfunctioning of its radar equipment and negligent navigation by a sailor led the destroyer to misread certain guiding signal lights, thus straying north into the Communist-controlled sea off Dongyin.

The PRC Navy dispatched eight Type 62 gunboats resulting in engagement at sea. The entire battle lasted 45 minutes. The destroyer was heavily damaged with seven deaths including its vice-Captain, and the commanding officer was seriously injured, along with over 40 sailors who sustained injury. The destroyer was towed back to port by other supporting warships that rushed to the scene. By then, the PRC gunboats had returned to their bases with two gunboats sustaining some damage. All this happened off the coast of Dongyin and thus it has been called the "Dongyin Sea Battle" ever since.

What's most surprising, or perhaps for seasoned political journalists not so surprising, is how Taiwan's Nationalist Navy as well as its media portrayed the battle at sea as a major victory, a tremendous feat in defeating a superior communist force. When they saw hardly any report from the Mainland media providing details of the encounter, the Nationalists found an opportunity to offer their own interpretation of the event to be used as a hype to booster morale, something of utmost political importance during those heady days. They claimed that four gunboats were sunk and two heavily damaged in the sea battle.

Ancient anti-aircraft gun / 古老炮台
Bunkers on Dongyin / 東引島的碉堡

Pix of YouTube film / YouTube 影片畫面
"Victory" celebration / 凱旋慶典

Despite the navigation error and an obvious defeat, the Captain was decorated and promoted, likewise many of the boat's officers and sailors, who were featured as national heroes. Later, a major event with over two thousand spectators was organized to cheer the return of the warship to the south. A film online today shows the victory celebration with bouquets of flowers offered to the officers and crew. For me, it offers food for thought, of how political or military reports are often subject to manipulation rather than providing fact and transparency, be it from the communist or nationalist.

Today, over fifty years after the episode, historians are allowed to scrutinize the military records of both Taiwan and the Mainland, and have come to admit the variance between reporting and fact. But this is more than half a century after the Dongjiang destroyer sustained 154 rounds of injury and was shot up to the front page of the news.

I had heard that Dongyin was a military fortress for Taiwan's northern fringes and visitors were not allowed on it until only a couple years ago, when détente between the Mainland and Taiwan seemed to be established. More than once, I attempted to be one of the first outsiders to visit the island, but each time it was futile. Now I have pre-booked a home-stay hostel and even reserved a scooter for me to get around.

My anxiety was running high when the Taima ferry made a stop the following morning at Matsu Islands before heading onward to Dongyin. Were my hopes to be dashed once again? The purser on the boat knocked at my cabin door and introduced himself. My booking for the return journey in two days' time had been canceled. They were expecting high wind and big waves at sea, thus the ferry would stop running for at least one week after arriving and would leave Dongyin before noon. I could stay and wait indefinitely for the ferry to start again or return to Keelung with the boat. One minor consolation prize - the purser told me that the ferry would stop at port for two hours so I might step ashore for a stroll.

Stroll I did. As soon as we arrived at port at 6:20am, I called to cancel my room booking and scooter. Meanwhile I joined the passengers off, all locals with a few fishing enthusiasts with gear, followed by scooters and cars. We disembarked off the front end of the Taimar ferry, as the boat can open on both bow and stern like a landing craft. There was a quick travel document check and I was out on the harbor causeway street.

First came to sight inside the harbor was a huge sign in red advocating Unity and Loyalty, not unlike propaganda billboards visible on the Mainland a few decades ago, but today replaced by commercial advertising. An egret stood peacefully on a small fishing boat as I approached, a sign of how peaceful the island had become. Most fishing vessels had, as tradition dictated, two eyes painted under the bow, in order to bring luck and promote visibility at sea.

At such early hours, only one café was open, with the name of "Stamina Breakfast". One young lady was behind the kitchen counter and I ordered my simple breakfast of egg with sausage and milk tea. Just as I was sitting down, five or six young guests came through the door, each with a dog on leash. They turned out to be a morning

Sign & egret / 紅標與白鷺
Outing for the blind / 失明人士的外遊

gathering of the deaf-mate community. From the smiles and delight on their faces, such gathering of those with the same disability gave them joy and mutual encouragement. I ate my breakfast and observed quietly from a corner.

As I finished breakfast, I walked out and paced the causeway of the harbor. A small fishing boat sped in and docked next to me. On it was a middle-age man in waterproof long johns. Immediately, he got down to work, untying loads of fish from his net, separating them and putting them into several buckets. Soon these buckets were full of fish of various types. In about ten minutes his job was completed and he brought to shore four bucket loads of fish.

Momentarily, a young lady on a scooter arrived at the dock and the man attached two buckets full of fish, one on each side of the scooter. The lady turned around and drove off towards the market, as I learned when I began a conversation with the man. He was hurrying to finish his work as he hauled the two remaining buckets with seawater and live fish inside a large building adjacent to the dock. This turned out to have several seafood restaurants inside and he proceeded to pour the live fish into tanks. These would be served up later in the day as locals or visitors stopped for their lunch or dinner

By now I had been on shore for well over an hour and passengers had started arriving to board the Taimar once again. I had a cup of latte at the Starbucks Café, by then open, before rushing back to walk up the plank into my now well-acquainted ferry boat. A line of military trucks parked by the Taima were obviously there to deliver supplies to troops on the island.

A tug boat came to our side to push the Taimar off its docking. The Taimar left the port of Dongyin at 11am and the journey back would take around eight hours, arriving in time for me to have dinner at Keelung. As our ferry left port, I saw the many artillery installations and bunkers around the south and west side of the island silhouetting against the beautiful coastal rock formation. Despite such signs of danger, the ocean was calm and I again sat near the chimney to reminisce on my old school days.

I took a peek into the bridge where the captain was looking blankly into the ocean rather than mastering and steering the ferry. Later when I checked again, to my great surprise, no one was inside the bridge area as the Taimar was sailing the vast ocean as if on auto pilot. I could only hope that this momentary lapse of a sea captain, or his run for the toilet, would not trigger another unwanted sea battle if we were to mistakenly steer into

Fresh catch / 新鮮漁獲

Military convoy / 軍事護衛

dangerous ground.

Later evening set in, and I watched a most spectacular sunset as we crossed paths with gigantic container ships on the major sea lane off the coast of Taiwan. It was all dark when the lights of Keelung finally showing up in the distance as we sailed into Keelung harbor. It may seem unbecoming that I should write about Dongyin after only a two-hour stay. But when I think of Samuel Beckett's play Waiting for Godot, who never showed up, or Peter Mattheissen's book The Snow Leopard, which was never seen during two years of searching, then my two-hour visit after my endless pursuit seems to more than justify this short piece.

Container at sea / 海上的貨櫃船

島嶼尋訪

卸不下的焦慮與不安

我站在渡輪尾艙，靠近煙囪的甲板上。身心都感受一份暖意，一份深埋心中超過半世紀之久——幾乎早已不復記憶的懷鄉之情，頃刻間竟被喚起。

深夜時分，我正在往返基隆與馬祖的「臺馬之星」渡輪上，車輛都在底層艙裡，我們剛從台灣最北端的基隆港出發，往大海開去。這艘啟用了四年的船，重達五千噸，船身長一百公尺。但此刻我的一顆心卻飄向另一顆「星」，那是香港的「天星小輪」，約一百六十噸重的船，長度僅「臺馬之星」的三分之一。不知為何，那段青澀年少的歲月，像浪潮般，倏忽湧上心頭。

一九六一至六七年間長達六年，當時正值十二至十八歲的我，總喜歡在冬季時分緊倚著香港渡輪底層近煙囪處的位子坐，跨海到九龍尖沙咀再到旺角的高中上學。我偶爾會帶著那台具十段變速的腳踏車一起搭船過海，六十年代的香港，有那樣一台酷炫的 *BSA* 腳踏車是很拉風的，格外吸睛。不過，「天星小輪」提供的位子比較高檔，連提貨上船都不准了，遑論一台腳踏車；所以，若要帶上腳踏車，我就得選搭沒那麼豪華舒適的「油麻地渡輪」，從灣仔出發到佐敦道。

雖然渡輪煙囪輸送引擎熱氣，但下層座位屬開放式空間，沒有窗戶阻擋凜冽北風，加

上羽絨外套既不盛行也買不起，身上的校服和我年少的身型一樣單薄，抵不住四面八方的刺骨寒風，吹得我特別難受。

當年的渡輪價位，上層座位一張票要價港幣兩毫，下層座位則便宜一半。值得一提的是，一九六六年，就在我會考前一年，「天星小輪」還曾因為漲價而引發了一場市民上街抗議的暴動。調整後的福利政策讓我們這群未成年孩子受惠不少，不但船票價格下調，還開放下層空間，讓小販提著籃子上船兜售零食；而上層船艙乘客則大多是西裝筆挺的紳士，與一身洋裝或已成絕響的優雅旗袍的女士。

HM next to Taima chimney /
「臺馬之星」煙囪旁的 HM

我成長於香港的中產家庭，家住銅鑼灣的大坑道。我就讀耶穌會成立的中學，就在香港對海半島上的九龍區，維多利亞港對岸；因此夏季時每週有五天搭船往返，冬天則多半天。那段週而復始的搭船與單車經驗，當時也滿足了我對外在世界探索的渴望。

此時當下，我就站在「臺馬之星」的甲板上，累了就倚坐在戶外椅上。這是我第三次從台灣北海岸出發前往東引島；第一次因船班時間更動而去不成，第二次則因颱風逼近而被迫放棄。

東引島包含三個小島，由堤壩型橋梁相連而成。島嶼面積還不足四點五平方公里，大約是香港長洲島的兩倍大。東引島是台灣最

Peddler of food / 路邊小食小販
Type 62 gunboat / 62 型護衛艇

北端的領土，有「國之北疆」之喻。為防中國大陸的軍事威脅，東引島曾是台灣的國防重鎮，據聞島上布滿巡航導彈，但在我抵達當地時，從遠處眺望，卻只看到幾個舊式防空高射砲。

一九六五年大概五十五年前的五月一日，台灣的國軍海防與中國海軍曾在東引島附近，爆發一場因誤會而引起的「五一海戰」。時值文革初期，中國媒體對此小規模戰鬥僅以小版面輕描淡寫一則誤闖中國海域的台籍船艦，與數個中國炮艇會戰的新聞事件。以當時中國的報導模式看來，如果媒體對此大肆報導，極有可能會被當成共產黨的宣傳素材。無論如何，台灣這一方則把當時的衝突視為大事，隨即引起西方媒體的關注與追蹤。

檢視事件始末，闖禍的「東江號」巡邏艦當時剛完成大整修，後被分派往北，直達最北端的東引島。海事衝突後，台灣國軍海防承認，導火線源於雷達系統的故障，與一名大意的海軍人員因誤判信號，而直驅入東引島以外的中國海域。中國海軍派出了八艘 62 型護衛艇，引發這場海上衝突。整場戰事歷時四十五分鐘，闖禍的巡邏艦嚴重受損，台灣方面包括副隊長在內總計七人陣亡，除了司令官受重傷外，另外四十名海軍官兵也負傷而退。隨後有船艦趕來護航援助，把「東江號」拖回港口；中國海軍的其中兩台炮艇也被彈擊，爾後全軍撤退返營。這一切發生在東引島沿海一帶，所以亦稱「東引海戰」。

台灣海軍與當時的媒體把這起海事衝突視為一場「擊敗共產大敵匪艇」的大勝利，或許對經驗老道的政治記者，如此虛張聲勢的報導見怪不怪，但仍令我詫異得難以置信。眼見中國對此海戰並未詳細見報，台灣軍方卻見機不可失而大書特書，聲稱共軍的四艘炮艦被擊沉而另兩艘則嚴重受損。看來，在那段動輒自我陶醉的非常年代，急需藉此提振政治士氣。

誤判信號的人為疏失被掩飾，明確被擊敗的實況也隻字未提，海軍艦長與其他船艦軍官倒是因此而被晉升與形塑成國民英雄。不久，政府便舉辦了一場超過兩千群眾的隆重慶典，夾道歡迎凱旋歸來的戰艦。今天在網路上仍能看到這段「決勝回朝」的影片，記錄了熱情群眾以鮮花慶賀決戰海疆的軍官與士兵。我為此而思索良久——且不論共產黨或國民黨，政治或戰事報導是如何一步步淪為操弄工具，而喪失了「報導透明、表述真相」的媒介使命？

Yaumati Ferry / 油麻地小輪

今天，事過境遷已逾五十年，歷史學家可以重新檢視台灣與中國雙方的軍事報導，並坦承雙方確實對海戰實況各自表述，落差甚大。但這起事件造成一百五十四人輕重傷、還被當頭版頭條處理的新聞報導，畢竟是超過半世紀前的戰事了。我知道東引島曾是台灣「國之北疆」的軍事要塞，謝絕觀光客踏足，一直到台灣與大陸的緊張關係趨緩，前幾年才逐步對外開放。我多希望自己能成為最先登島的數人之一，但每一次都因故生變，計劃付諸東流。這一次我已預訂了民宿與可以載我四處環島的機車。

隔日清晨，當「臺馬之星」停靠馬祖島時，我心中騰升一股憂驚：不會吧？我殷切的期待又要落空了嗎？有人敲門，是船務長。他告訴我，我兩天後的回程已被取消。根據氣象，未來海上有強風大浪，所以，渡輪會在這次抵達東引島後回基隆停靠當地，停駛一週；換句話說，這艘渡輪會在風浪來襲前的當日中午，從東引島返回基隆。我可以跟著渡輪到東引島，遙遙無期地等待風雨暫歇後，再等著大船到後離開；或跟著大家當天返回基隆。小小的安慰獎是——船務長安撫我，渡輪將停靠東引島兩小時，所以，或許我可以下船，「踏足」東引，走馬看花散散步。

我當然選擇「登島」漫步。大船清晨六點二十分抵達東引島，我致電取消住宿與機車預訂。同時跟著乘客下船，當地人中有些一看就是裝備整齊的垂釣者，不少機車與車子呼嘯而過。「臺馬之星」渡輪像登陸艇一樣，首尾兩端都可開啟，我們在前端下船。入口處有個「快易通」的文件檢查站，不稍一會兒，我便走在港口的防堤街道上了。

進入眼簾的是一幅巨型壁報，醒目的紅標鼓吹「忠誠團結」，不就像十幾年前在中國大陸隨處可見的愛國宣傳？而今，許多類似公告都被商業廣告取而代之了。往前走，

眼前一張壁畫，一隻白鷺不驚不擾地站在一艘小釣艇上，讓人感覺，曾經軍令如山之地，已轉型為平靜祥和、可親可近的小島。許多漁船在船頭漆上一雙眼，當地民間傳統相信，此舉可讓出航一帆風順，也能提升海上能見度，不至觸礁。

一大早，只有一家咖啡館開門營業，「元氣早餐」咖啡館。年輕女士躲在廚房櫃檯後方，我點了雞蛋配香腸與奶茶的簡單早餐。我才一坐下，隨即來了五六位年輕客人，各人手上緊牽著狗。原來是一群聾啞社群的早晨聚會。我坐在餐廳角落，邊吃早餐邊安靜觀察。他們臉上掩不住笑意，或許同為身心障礙者的感同身受，讓他們因相互鼓舞而喜不自勝。吃完早餐，我走到港口街道上。一艘小漁船剛進港，就停靠我身邊。

一名中年男人在船上，身穿整套防水衣褲，手腳利落地下船工作，把一整網漁獲解開，分類裝進數個桶子裡。不一會兒，桶子已裝滿各種魚。十分鐘內便大功告成，將裝滿魚的四個桶子帶上岸。一轉身，便見一年輕女子騎著機車抵達碼頭，那男人把兩桶漁獲放上機車，女子轉頭就往市場騎去。男人繼續埋頭趕工，一邊告訴我，他得將另外兩桶裝滿海水與生猛的漁獲，送到碼頭附近的一間大樓去。原來大樓裡有好幾間海鮮餐廳，他要將這群活潑亂跳的活魚倒入餐廳的水族箱裡。稍晚用餐時間到，當地人與遊客便將陸續過來享用午餐或晚餐。

我到處遊蕩了超過一小時，「臺馬」渡輪的乘客陸續回到碼頭，準備上船。重返熟悉的大船之前，我先到星巴克點了杯拿鐵，坐在那兒正好瞥見停靠渡輪旁的軍用卡車，準備把運來的物資送往島上的軍營。

一艘大拖船緩緩過來，將「臺馬」渡輪推離船塢。大船於十一點準時離開東引島，全程要再八小時

才能抵達基隆，剛好趕得及返回基隆吃晚餐。出發離港時，我看見島嶼南方被大炮裝置與軍事地堡圍繞，而島嶼西邊的輪廓，則在海濱礁石的堆砌下，襯托出小島迤邐風光的一面。儘管這些軍事裝置令人難免不安，但眼前無邊無際的大海平靜無波，我再度坐到靠近煙囪的位子，任由思緒將我帶回那段搭船上下學的舊日時光裡。

我往船長駕駛室窺探，竟看到船長一臉茫然望向大海，毫沒掌舵之勢。我稍後再查看一次，這下更令我驚詫不已了，駕駛室內竟連個人影也沒有，而「臺馬」渡輪就這樣仿若自動駕駛般，在汪洋大海中持續前進。我只能暗自希望，不管船長是人有三急不得不衝廁所或其他緣由，千萬不可讓他的一時疏忽大意而把我們連人帶船，誤闖危險海域而引發另一場不必要的海事戰亂。

傍晚時分，當我們與另一艘超級貨運在大海上擦肩而過時，夕陽餘暉下，落日熔金的壯美景致在我眼前鋪展開來。海天漆黑一片，只有在我們逐漸往基隆港靠近時，最終從遠處瞥見點點燈火。或許只待東引島兩小時不足以完整書寫描繪這個島嶼，這讓我想起山繆·貝克特 (Samuel Beckett) 的《等待果陀》，或彼得·馬修森 (Peter Matthiessen) 的《雪豹：一個自然學家的性靈探索之旅》，無論是始終不曾出現的果陀，或耗費兩年亦從未尋得的雪豹，相較之下，我三番兩次亟欲登島尋訪的努力，最終換來兩小時的「腳踏實地」，已讓我有足夠的理由來完成這篇短文。

Sunset into ocean / 日落海洋

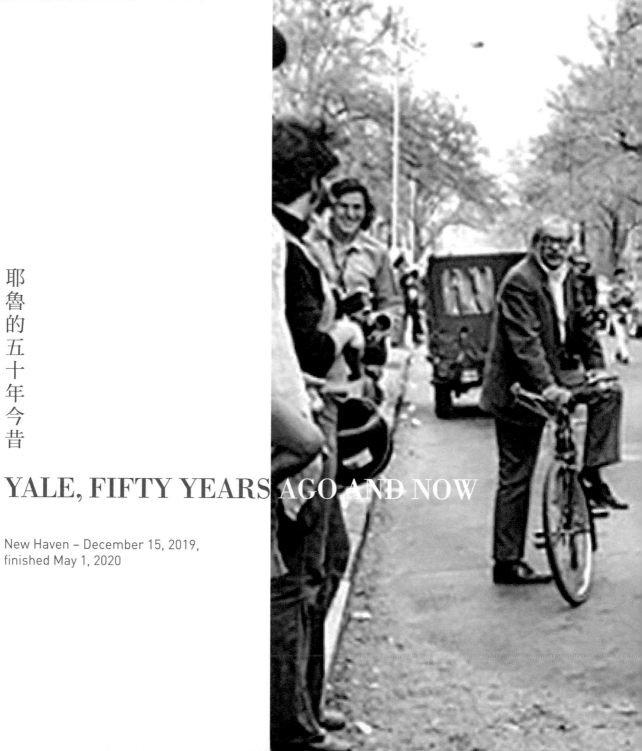

耶
魯
的
五
十
年
今
昔

YALE, FIFTY YEARS AGO AND NOW

New Haven – December 15, 2019,
finished May 1, 2020

YALE, FIFTY YEARS AGO AND NOW

"You know, there used to be a phone booth inside our house," quips Helen. "Oh yeah? Zoe, your daughter, told me this was the former publishing house of Human Relations Area File, HRAF, when she saw the ethnographic monograph on Tibetan nomads I assigned for her to read," I answer.

"Yes, but that's later on. All three houses, one on each of our sides, were base for the OSS during and after the War, recruiting agents and officers from Yale, and they needed privacy and secrecy when speaking on the phone to the outside," adds Helen. Surely the OSS, or Office of Strategic Services founded by Bill Donovan, the mother of the CIA, would need a little privacy. There is even a book, Cloak and Gown: Scholars in the Secret War, 1939-1961, about America's secret service among academics. In it, authored by a Yale professor of History, large sections are devoted to the target of Yale in recruitment, not unlike the UK's MI5 and MI6, with their focus on Cambridge University. The practice was so prevalent that some students may feel slighted if not approached by the recruiters to join the elitist group.

Helen is the wife of Professor Barry Nalebuff, and their daughter Zoe was our gap year intern ten years ago when she left Choate and before she started her degree at the University of Chicago. On this trip, I am taking up her room, since both daughters have long since left home and are now living in New York. The train ride from New York took just two hours, but my last trip here, 50 years ago in the spring of 1970, took a good couple days, hitchhiking with a hippie friend from Wisconsin to Connecticut.

At that time half a century ago, I was a freshman studying Journalism and Art at the University of Wisconsin at River Falls, a short distance across the State line from St Paul/Minneapolis, Minnesota. Campus was on and off in turmoil as students and professors protested against the Vietnam War. Some of my friends rallying against the War were veterans who had just returned from Vietnam and were going to university on the GI Bill. Both journalism and art schools were not known for being conservative, and both faculty and students were very much caught up in the anti-War movements. As a foreign student, I was more apprehensive and, though my sentiments were not radical, I certainly was on the progressive side along with my fellow classmates.

This was the first of several hitchhiking experiences during my college years. John my hippie friend from Eugene Oregon looked like Jesus and spoke with a muffled voice, filtered through his long beard with matching long hair. It was through him that I learned that "Jesus Christ" was not just

Barry's house / 貝利的大宅
Guards opposite students / 警衛隊與學生對立

a noun, but also an exclamation! The length of my hair was not far behind his, and in those days many teenagers with their beard looked like old men. From New Haven, I would catch a bus to New York where my sister was. John, however, was into a very different agenda. He was at New Haven to join the May Day protest. Many different civic and civil groups, among them Yale students, the Black Panthers from Chicago and their supporters, joined during the days leading up to May 1, when the big rally was supposed to take place. I wasn't there to witness the unfolding fiasco and melee, but did follow the development as things unfolded in the news.

The call to arms was because one of the original Chicago Eight was to be tried in New Haven. The Chicago Eight were later called the Chicago Seven, as the seven "whites" were acquitted, leaving the single "black," Bobby Seale, the cofounder of the militant Black Panthers, to face trial. My narrative here is of course a simplified and concise summary of a very complex cause that dated back through years if not decades of the civil rights movement, mixed in with a more immediate anti-war movement.

Not only the police and the FBI, but the National Guard as well were called in, as sentiments rose to boiling point and anticipation was high for things to turn into ugly riots. Heavily armed with tear gas masks and fixed bayonets with sheaths off, the Guards would march forward in rows to disperse the gathering protesters. Tear gas was considered run-of-the-mill stuff.

Though May Day New Haven turned out to be relatively peaceful in the end, four days later on May 4 was the Kent State University confrontation between students and the National Guard. Four *students were shot dead. That episode triggered nation-wide discord, protests and shut downs of schools and universities across the country. I recalled sit-ins and protests across campuses during the following months leading to our university having no final examinations, substituting our mid-term grades as final.*

But looking back at the heavy-handedness of US government response during those heady days bears witness and contrasts to what happened recently in my hometown of Hong Kong. What started as political protest there turned into civil unrest and then outright riots. Firebombs were everywhere and public facilities were vandalized. By comparison, the Hong Kong police, despite operating under extreme duress and other constraints, acted with great restraint.

As expected, the media, including newspapers, television channels and internet news were divided, based on a divisive political line. What surprised me as a former frontline journalist for the National Geographic, as well as having been featured on CNN over a dozen times, was how the western media chose their line of reporting on a totally lop-sided and selective coverage, barely if at all featuring the extremist behavior of the protesters while smearing the Hong Kong government, in particular the world-acclaimed HK Police force. Yet I can fully understand the bigger picture globally among western media eager to join the uniform China-bashing agenda opposing the country's rise, with Hong Kong no doubt being a corollary to that new trend.

The swarm of so-called "reporters" during the 2019 Hong Kong riots right into center of the crossfire as well as serving as frontline buffer for the protesters is unheard of in any previous skirmishes between police and rioters, not least during the Hong Kong 1967 riots when I was graduating from high school. It raises doubts in my own mind of why I needed to spend three quarters at journalism school to study Press Law, including an independent quarter going through case studies of Press Law in Britain and Hong Kong at a law office belonging to my father's friend. Noted Barrister Patrick Yu was a classmate of my father both at Wah Yan, a high school run by Irish Jesuits, and later at Hong Kong University while staying at Ricci Hall.

Those who proclaimed the loudest in the name of freedom and democracy in Hong Kong had never seen or even heard of the long history of rights movements and their confrontation in the US. One of my standard reads as a journalism student was Bury my Heart at Wounded Knee, about the history of the American West and the oppression and extermination of Native Americans. In much of the world, such struggles go on, as history attests. Politicians will continue to be best in maneuvering and inciting their followers, whether their agendas are real or packaged as real.

New Haven and Yale today is a very different scene, quiet as college campuses go given that the school term has ended and Christmas holidays started. I arrive at the New Haven train station mid-afternoon. Helen is on hand to pick me up and drives me to her house. Husband Barry, the professor, is supposed to be landing around the same time, returning from Beijing after his year of lecturing at the Schwarzman College of Qinghua University. Barry is a Chaired Professor at Yale, teaching game theory at the Business School, specializing on the strategy of negotiation. Helen meanwhile leaves for an art opening at a non-profit gallery she founded some years ago here in New Haven.

By late afternoon, Barry comes through the door while I am reading from his pile of books on the ground in boxes, among tennis shoes and ping pong balls and paddles. China airlines has lost his

Display of Bobby Seale / 巴比·希爾的海報展示　　　May Day at Yale / 耶魯大學的五月天

luggage, but these days such matters can usually be reconciled within a day or two. Together we leave for the gallery opening.

After staying for about an hour, we walk over to his friend's studio home which is hosting a cocktail reception for the artists and guests. Hung on the wall inside the semi-open bedroom is a portrait of Bobby Seale, apparently an icon even to this day at Yale, not unlike Che Guevara in many parts of the world. A couple of drinks later, we bow out, citing jetlag, and go to a tiny Japanese restaurant.

Ordering a set dinner, we chat as I update Barry on some of our recent projects, with portfolio now expanding well beyond China. Barry is totally fluent in Putonghua or Mandarin Chinese, having lived in Shanghai many years ago. As we rise to leave, Barry introduces me to a husband and wife sitting at the Sushi Bar. Professor William Nordhaus lives just two houses down from Barry's home.

Nordhaus is an economist who won the Nobel Prize in Economics just a year ago in 2018 for his study of the macroeconomics of climate change. At the time when the prize was announced, he was surprised that he co-shared the prize with another economist rather than with his former colleague, someone who later joined Harvard and who coincidentally just committed suicide less than four months ago. Having myself been a neighbor of another famous Nobel laureate, I take notice whenever I meet such distinguished individuals. When I was residing in the US in a mountain cabin in the Angeles National Forest above Pasadena, Richard Feynman, one of the most admired Nobel physicists, was a weekend neighbor, owning one of the houses among 14 cabins inside the nature reserve.

I am also hoping to visit David Swensen, renowned Chief Investment Officer of the Yale Endowment. But his recovery from cancer probably precludes his seeing a stranger except the most intimate and closest of friends. David was two years behind me as an undergraduate at the University of Wisconsin and his father Richard Swensen was my Dean when I attended college. Both "Dick" Swensen and his wife Grace were very close to me. They drove to the university long after retirement to meet me on two occasions, first when I received the Distinguished Alumni Award and later an Honorary Doctorate. Dick even procured two autographed books from David to me. David Swensen is indeed one of the most admired professors at Yale and has a following among financial investment circles throughout the world. Yale of course has many such distinguished scholars and alumni.

One such person less known to me as being a Yale graduate is Sir Norman Foster, a Pritzker Prize architect. It isn't until the following day when Barry takes me to his office that I realize the four-year-old and very posh School of Management at Yale was designed by this world-renowned architect. Barry takes me on a nice tour inside the building before stopping at his corner office. Up *against the long windows are not books, but a long line of beverage bottle specimens.*

Barry is no passive academic at Yale. With one of his former students, he co-founded Honest Tea after he deemed all other tea available in the market too sweet. After a decade of set backs and turns of fortune, Honest Tea became a "must have" for health-concerned individuals and its multiple-flavored teas were well stocked at all the healthier supermarkets and convenience stores. Obama's White House was said to have kept a regular supply. It finally became so successful that it was ultimately bought out by Coca-Cola, which was eager to enter the health drink market. A wonderfully drawn graphic novel, Mission in a Bottle, tells tales about the ordeals and triumph of Barry and his student Seth.

Right outside Barry's office and next to the elevator is something else unusual at a Business School. Barry has set up a Ping Pong table adjacent to his room. I had played in the university team some 50 years ago and Barry is eager to challenge yours truly to a game. We do a few volleys and I know my old skills have long since left me. Rather than playing formally, I decide to just play a casual twenty minutes practice, so as to save Barry the trouble of picking up balls all over the place. At home, I practice occasionally at my studio, playing against a machine with 150 balls served

National Forest Cabin / 國家森林木屋

out one after another.

Before I leave on a late afternoon train back to New York, Barry rushes me to visit the Yale Peabody Museum of Natural History. It is within five- minutes' walk from his house. The famous dinosaur specimens are supposed to be soon dismantled, making room for total rebuilding of a new museum. With less than an hour to my train's departure, Barry, demonstrates his skill at management and maximizing return, squeezing in time to make a quick walk-through the Yale University Art Museum. He tries in vain to find the wing with an exhibit of Chinese ethnic minority costumes. With the help of the guards, we manage to stop there for a quick look for ten short minutes.

The clock is ticking, yet we stop for a moment in front of the Thinker sculpture by Rodin. Facing it is perhaps the most highly prized and priced among the art collection of Yale, the Night Cafe of Van Gogh. I stand in awe appreciating the vibrant colors of orange and yellow, with a pool table rather than a ping pong table. Suddenly I realize coincidentally Barry is a great complement to the Van Gogh piece, as he is, totally by chance, wearing matching yellow and orange colors.

So what if I miss the train. There would always be another within the hour.

Dinosaur exhibit at Peabody Museum / 展於「皮博迪博物館」的恐龍標本
Minority Costumes at Art Museum / 展於藝術博物館的少數民族服裝

CEREMONIAL DRESS FROM SOUTHWEST CHINA

THE ANN B. GOODMAN COLLECTION

耶魯的五十年今昔

「你知道嗎，我們的房子裡原來有個電話亭，」海倫俏皮地說。「哦，真的？有一次當你女兒佐伊看到我指定她閱讀 *HRAF* 出版的有關西藏牧民的民族誌時，她告訴過我，她家房子的前身正是『人類關係區域檔案』*(Human Relations Area Files, HRAF)* 的出版社。」我回答。

「是啊，但那是之後了。之前這裡所有三間房子都是世界大戰時期與戰後的『戰略情報局』駐地，進駐了面向耶魯的招募人員與軍官。當他們與外界講電話時，需要隱私和非常私密的空間。」海倫補充說道。可想而知，由中央情報局創始人威廉・唐諾文 *(William J. Donovan)* 所成立的「戰略情報局」，當然需要隱秘的空間。我還記得，有一本耶魯大學歷史系教授出的書《斗篷與長袍：密戰背後的學者 *1939-1961*》*(Cloak and Gown: Scholars in the Secret War, 1939-1961)*，甚至詳實敘述那些在美國學術界所提供的秘密服務，其中大部分以招募耶魯的成員為主，一如「英國安全局」的「軍情五處」與「軍情六處」也把焦點放在劍橋大學；這些計劃的執行如此普遍而令人欣羨，能被選上受邀加入精英團隊一員，對學生而言，都是無比榮幸的事。

海倫是耶魯大學教授貝利・奈勒柏夫 *(Barry Nalebuff)* 的妻子，而他們的女兒佐伊，十年前高中畢業後，在進入芝加哥大學升造前，曾到我們的學會實習半年。我在這段旅程中到他們家，就借住佐伊的臥室，姐妹倆都已離家好久，目前定居於紐約。其實，從

Fixed bayonets of Guards / 荷槍實彈的警衛隊

紐約搭火車到這裡只需兩小時，但我想起五十年前最後一次到此一遊時，是一九七零年的春天，我和一位嬉皮朋友一路搭順風車，耗了好多天才從威斯康辛州，輾轉來到康乃狄克州。

屈指一算，那已是半世紀前的事了。我當時是新聞與藝術雙主修的大一新生，威斯康辛大學的河瀑分校，州際邊界與明尼蘇達州的明尼阿波利斯-聖保羅都會區相鄰不遠。大學內的師生經常為了反越戰而頻頻在校園和上街頭抗議，紛擾動亂是常態。有些加入反戰示威遊行的朋友是剛從越南返美的退役軍人，以保障退役軍人福利的「美國軍人權利法案」之名，申請就讀大學；而我們大學的新聞系與藝術系，向來不見得保守，學系和學生也被捲入這場反戰運動，投入其中。身為外籍學生，如此情勢難免令我惴惴不安，雖然我本質上並不主張激進，但在這議題上，我義無反顧與我的同學們站在同一陣線。

大學期間，也是我人生中幾次搭便車的最初體驗。來自奧勒岡州的約翰，是我的嬉皮朋友，講起話來聲音低沉暗啞，長鬍鬚外加披肩長髮，看起來很像耶穌。我透過他才赫然知道，原來「耶穌基督」

不只是個名詞，同時也是個驚歎詞！我當時的頭髮長度其實和約翰不相上下，那時代的年輕人喜歡蓄長鬍，十足老頭子的模樣。到達東岸後，我從紐哈芬搭公車到紐約找我姐姐。而約翰的行程與計劃則大不相同。他待在紐哈芬是為了參加喧騰一時的「五月天抗爭」(May Day Protest) 的反戰運動；許多市民與民間組織包括耶魯的學生都積極參與其中，在芝加哥崛起的「黑豹黨」與其眾多支持者，更大張旗鼓地投入五月一日這場示威大遊行。那一次行動最終以一場混戰落幕，鎩羽而歸，我沒有親身見證，但也不斷從新聞媒體的報導中，持續關注後續的發展。

一場遊行轉為武裝隊伍，起因乃「芝加哥八人」的其中一員在紐哈芬被起訴審判；原有的「芝加哥八人」最後因這七名「白人」獲判無罪而成了「芝加哥七人」，唯獨其中一位「黑人」巴比‧希爾 (Bobby Seale) 被判刑。巴比之前成立了美國歷史上重要的黑人民兵團體「黑豹黨」，並成為黨主席。當然，我在這裡的文字敘述與總結都過於簡化，畢竟那是一段錯綜複雜、爭取人民權益長達數十年的行動，其中還參雜了迫在眉睫的反戰抗爭。

在現場維安的，除了警察與聯邦調查局以外，連國民警衛隊也被調召到遊行隊伍中支援，平和的訴求逐漸升溫，警民對峙的緊張情勢，最終演變成一發不可收拾的暴動。荷槍實彈的警衛隊戴上催淚瓦斯面罩，利刃脫鞘，明槍明劍，整齊排列地步步逼近，試圖一舉驅散示威者。警方派上用場的催淚瓦斯，已是最稀鬆平常的東西了。雖然這場紐哈芬的「五月天抗爭」最後還算和平落幕，但四天後的五月四日，在肯特州立大學一場涉及學生隊伍與國民警衛隊的衝突事件中，四名學生被槍殺身亡。這起事件彷若燎原之火，激化全國性的對立與仇恨，抗爭遊行頻傳，無數學校與大學也受波及而

關閉。我還記得就讀的大學，經常舉辦靜坐示威，如此連續了好幾個月，連期末考也取消，以期中成績取代。

回頭檢視美國政府在那段狂飆時期對示威民眾粗暴的鎮壓，見證並映照出近日在香港——我的家鄉所發生的類似事件。一切始於政治抗議，然後引發警民騷動，最終一觸即發，難以收拾，惡化成徹底對立，而爆發動亂。汽油彈無處不在，公共設施被蓄意破壞。兩相對照下，香港警察在強烈脅迫與其他限制下，算是高度克制了。

不出我所料，報紙、電視媒體與網媒，果然依照既有的政治立場，自我主張，各自表述。身為前《國家地理雜誌》的前線記者，我之前也曾數度被受訪問而刊載於「美國有線電視新聞網」上，因此，從新聞專業素養與經驗出發，當我看到西方媒體如何選邊站，幾乎不報導抗議人士的極端行為，卻一昧詆毀香港政府、醜化享譽國際的香港警力時，那樣徹底失衡的報導，仍令我訝然吃驚。雖然如此，我對西方媒體亟欲建構全球性的未來圖象——集體打壓中國崛起的企圖——我其實了然於心；而香港，無疑是這股新趨勢最理所當然的目標。

二零一九年香港暴動中，所謂「一群記者」衝入激烈對峙交鋒，或肉身擋在示威者前等情況，從不曾在外國警方與抗議民眾之間的衝突中發生，更未曾在我高中畢業的一九六七年香港動亂中出現過。這些報導令我困惑，也明白何以我需要在新聞學院用了三個學期的學程，來學習新聞法律，其中還包括一整個學期都泡在英國新聞法律的個案研究，還為此到父親朋友的香港法律事務所學習。當時，這位父執輩朋友是香港家喻戶曉的余叔韶大律師，與我父親是耶穌會「華仁書院」的中學同學，然後再一起到香港大學讀書，甚至還同宿於港大的利瑪竇宿舍。

那些在香港把「民主與自由」口號喊得震天價響的人，其實對美國境內漫長的人權運動與鬥爭歷史，從未見識或聽聞。當我還是新聞系學生時，其中一本必讀書籍是《魂歸傷膝谷》(*Bury My Heart at Wounded Knee*)，內容講述美國西部與印第安原住民之間，壓迫和對抗的歷史。歷史已經證實，類似的掙扎與動亂，恆常發生於世界各地。政客們持續竭盡所能地操弄與煽動追隨者，不管他們言之鑿鑿的目標是真心話，或只是包裝過的行銷術語。

今天的紐哈芬與耶魯，和過去喧鬧的形象，迥然有別；校園內安安靜靜，學期結束，聖誕假開始。我正中午時分抵達紐哈芬的火車站。海倫來接我，載我到她家。海倫的丈夫貝利·奈勒柏夫教授剛好也在同一時間從北京返回，他之前受邀到清華大學的蘇世民書院授課。貝利是耶魯大學的首席教授，在商學院教授賽局理論，協商談判策略是他專精的領域。而海倫則出門為一場藝術展開幕，地點就在她數年前於紐哈芬自創的非營利畫廊內。

Yale School of Management / 耶魯大學管理學院

Yale Peabody Museum / 耶魯大學「皮博迪博物館」

主人家的地上散置了裝滿書的箱子，就在運動鞋、乒乓球拍與划槳之間。午後，當我正閱讀這些書籍時，貝利開門入內。航空公司搞丟了他的行李，但現在這些行李遺失的事通常可以在一兩天內解決。我們一起出發到畫廊參加開幕展。

在那裡待了約一小時，我們走到他朋友的工作室，參與一場專為藝術家與賓客準備的雞尾酒會。半開放的臥室牆上，高掛「黑豹黨」靈魂人物巴比·希爾的肖像，顯然他至今仍是耶魯的指標性人物，一如切·格瓦拉在世人心中難以撼動的偶像地位。淺酌幾杯，我們便以時差理由提早離席，到一間小日本餐廳去。

點了晚餐，我向貝利提起近期的一些計劃，展示許多擴展至中國以外的作品集。貝利多年前曾在上海定居過，說得一口流利的普通話(華語)。正當我們準備離開時，貝利將我介紹給坐在壽司吧檯的一對夫妻，先生是威廉·諾德豪斯 (William Nordhaus) 教授，他們和貝利是僅相隔兩間房子的鄰居。

諾德豪斯是著名經濟學家，也是二零一八年諾貝爾經濟學獎得主，鑽研氣候變遷的宏觀經濟學。得知自己與另一位經濟學者一同獲頒諾貝爾獎時，諾德豪斯非常驚訝，他原以為與他共享這份獎項的，應是他的前同事；這位前同事後來從耶魯轉戰哈佛，四個月前自殺離世。我自己也曾與諾貝爾獎得主毗鄰而居，所以，

Receiving hug from Grace Swensen /
接受蕾絲·史雲生的擁抱

每一次有機會認識這些世界級的傑出人士，總能引起我的特別關注。我曾在美國加州帕薩迪納 (Pasadena) 的安琪拉國家森林 (Angeles National Forest) 的山區木屋裡，住過近十年的一段時日，享譽國際的諾貝爾物理獎得主理查·費曼 (Richard Feynman)，是森林保育區十四間木屋的其中一個屋主，也是我的週末鄰居。

我也滿心期待能去拜訪耶魯大學首席投資官大衛·史雲生 (David Swensen)，這位操盤手將耶魯的校務基金投資配置成功，豐功偉業使他一舉成名天下。但他當時剛從癌症復原不久，除非是極親近的朋友，否則大病初癒的他，一律婉拒訪客。大衛·史雲生在我就讀威斯康辛大學時，比我低兩屆，而他的父親李察·史雲生則是我當時的訓育主任。李察（迪克）·史雲生與其妻格蕾絲，和我是相識已久的老友。我一直記得他們夫妻倆在退休後，兩度開車到大學來和我會面，前後兩次分別是我獲頒「傑出校友」與榮譽博士學位的場合。迪克還特別跟大衛要了兩本親筆簽名的著作送我，大衛不僅是耶魯大學備受景仰的教授，也是聞名遐邇的投資大師；當然，耶魯向來不乏頂尖學者專家與傑出校友。

耶魯碩士畢業生中，我原來對諾曼·福斯特 (Norman Foster) 爵士所知不多，直到隔天貝利帶我到他辦公室時，我才赫然發現，原來耶魯那棟剛蓋好四年、典雅不俗的管理學院，是出自這位普立茲克建築獎得主的設計。貝利當起了我的建築導覽員，帶我到室內參觀，欣賞全球最具影響力的建築大師之大作。享受了一趟建築美學導覽之後，我們再一起到貝利位於轉角的辦公室。緊靠長長窗戶邊的架上，擺放的不是書，而是一整排的飲品空瓶。

貝利從來是個劍及履及，行動力十足的學者。當他確認市場上販售的茶飲糖分都偏高，便著手和一位畢業生自創「誠實茶」的健康茶品牌。經過起伏跌宕的市場歷練與十年磨劍，「誠實茶」如今已成為養生人士「必買」的健康茶，貝利師生研發的多種口味茶飲，也早已「佈局」各大小市場，包括健康超市與便利商店；據說連歐巴馬的白宮也指定要「常備」這款茶飲，確保供貨不斷。「誠實茶」熱銷到引起可口可樂的注意，最終決定全資收購，期待藉此踏入健康飲品的市場。一本圖象書籍《瓶中使命》(Mission in a Bottle)，完整敘述貝利與學生賽斯 (Seth) 這段歷經考驗與旗開得勝的創業歷程。

走出貝利的辦公室，我在電梯旁發現了另一個與商學院「招牌」有些違和的東西——一張乒乓桌。我曾是大學桌球校隊隊員，不過那已是五十年前的事了，只是，一旁的貝利已摩拳擦掌，迫不及待想與鄙人一較高下。我們一來一往地隨意玩了幾球，頓覺自己的技能已大不如前。不正式開戰了，我決定和貝利輕鬆練習二十分鐘就好，讓貝利省省力，不好意思讓他滿場彎腰撿球！我若沒有外出，偶爾也會在自己的工作室對著機器練球，一場下來，至少可以廝殺個一百五十球。

準備搭火車返回紐約的那個午後，貝利急著要帶我參觀耶魯大學的「皮博迪自然史博物館」(Peabody Museum of Natural History)，距

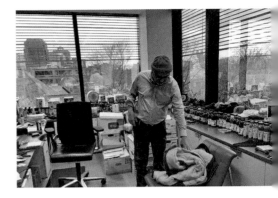

Barry's office with Honest Tea /
貝利辦公室的「誠實茶」

離他家只有五分鐘步行路程。博物館最著名的恐龍標本即將拆除，保留更多空間給整棟新館的重建。我的火車一小時後就要出發，貝利再把他擅長的管理技能，發揮得淋漓盡致，時間節奏掌握得滴水不漏，急匆匆地把我帶到耶魯大學的藝術博物館，要讓我看看中國少數民族的服裝展示；後來由警衛指點迷津，我們終於找到目標，駐足觀賞了十分鐘。

時鐘滴答不停走，我們見縫插針，在羅丹的「沉思者」銅雕前，停留片刻。當我站在梵谷畫作《夜間咖啡館》前，我思忖良久，能在耶魯大學的眾多藝術品中看見這幅名畫，那或許是最值回票價、也最無憾的事。梵谷式的黃色與橘色交織出絢麗斑斕的鮮明色彩，教人忍不住讚歎……哦，畫中擺放的是檯球桌，不是乒乓桌……。轉身無意間發現身旁的貝利，他當天隨意搭配的穿著，一身的黃色與橘色，竟無意間為梵谷致上了最高敬意，「天衣」無縫。

既已無憾，就算趕不上火車，也沒什麼大不了！反正再一小時內，下一班火車就來了。

Rodin's The Thinker / 羅丹的「沉思者」
Barry with Van Gogh / 貝利與梵高

緬
北
飛
地

NORTHERN MYANMAR ENCLAVE

Putao, Myanmar – January 21, 2020

NORTHERN MYANMAR ENCLAVE

"Relatives from Sawalong (Cawarong) invited us to visit. So, four years ago, I and six others took the 18-day trek across six mountains to reach the distant town in Tibet," said Huruq who is one of two Tibetan families now living in Sanlum Dam village on the eastern edge of Putao.

The long hike must have been exhausting for Huruq who is now seventy and was born in Myanmar. His father had moved approximately a century ago from Sawalong to northernmost Myanmar where there are now four Tibetan villages, Tawundam, Samdam, MaDein and Htaondam with about 200 Tibetan inhabitants in total. They say they are of the Drolpa tribe, historically living close to Sawalong.

"By car we all went to Kunming, and our relatives then took us all the way to Beijing," Huruq spoke with sparkles in his eyes, while his long face and deep features revealed his Tibetan heritage. The trip must have been quite an eye-opener for someone from one of the remotest corners of the world.

His daughter Sana Lamu and son-in-law Dorji had moved down the hill to the plain some four years ago. But during the spring and summer, they go back to high country. While we were chatting,

Dorji was busy preparing some salted butter tea for us, using a plastic churner rather than the traditional wooden cylinder churner.

A year ago, I was island-hopping at the southern tip of Myanmar in the Mergui Archipelagos when word arrived by satellite phone that my ageing father had taken a fall and I must turn back and rush to the hospital. A year later now and I'm in Putao, the northernmost region of Myanmar, exploring a valley surrounded by mountains, India to the west, China's Yunnan to the east, and Tibet to the north.

The left or west tributary of the Irrawaddy, called the Malikha, flows through the valley. Hkakabo Razi, known as the highest peak (5742 meters) in Myanmar until a recent contender peak Gamlang Razi knocked it out of the top spot, appears on the GPS app map. Both peaks are part of the eastern Himalayas, weeks away by trek through jungle and mountains.

Several attempts were made to summit Hkakapo Razi, with a Japanese and a Tibetan making the first successful ascent in 1996. Subsequent climbs resulted in death of two Burmese expedition members who disappeared during their descent. Mark Jenkins, a correspondent friend from Wyoming who was a member of one of the assaults, is seeking permission to climb it again in order to verify its height.

Putao Airport / 葡萄縣機場
Huruq, Tibetan of Myanmar / 住在緬甸的西藏人哈魯

Lamu and child / 拉姆與孩子
Rawang migration map / 日旺族遷徙地圖

Putao during WWII was known to Hump pilots as Fort Hertz, no doubt named by a former British colonialist. It was here that a radio station was set up, providing crucial radio signal for flyers with bearings to navigate across the hazardous eastern Himalayas, bringing equipment and supplies for wartime China. Over 600 airplanes (dubious reports boasted 2,000) were lost during a period of slightly over three years. CERS is fortunate to retain in our collection rare sheets of double-sided silk maps of Burma and the Hump - very finely printed dating from the War years in 1942 and 1944. I have brought them along as my guide.

My other guide for the last few days is Ram Sengh of Rawang ethnicity. They are the main ethnic group of Putao valley. Though only 28 years of age, he has trekked to the border with India, a thirteen-day hike crossing as many mountains westward, and to Tibet, a six-day journey north, as well as crossing into Yunnan, an eight-day trek crossing six mountains to the east. His most recent expedition was last November - a trek to the Dulong (Drung) River valley, trading for his family. They sell to China musk, cordyceps and at times bear gall, returning with more fashionable clothes and shoes. A musk pod, the dried scent gland of the male musk deer, can fetch five to six thousand Renminbi depending on its size. Ram Sengh used as point of departure Dazung Dam, his birth home, which is at an elevation of 1300 meters above sea level and a week's trek north of Putao.

His crossing point into China was exactly where I also crossed in 2016, though heading in the opposite direction, at Border Post 41 where the upper Irrawaddy, called Drung locally, flows from China into Myanmar. We compared our pictures of the final crossing and they corresponded perfectly. On the Myanmar side, the ethnic group called Rawang is the same as China's Dulong nationality. Story had it that when representatives of China's minority nationalities converged in Beijing in the 1950s, they got to meet with Chairman Mao. When a local from the Drung River saw Mao, the Chairman asked where he was from. He answered Drung and from then on the group became known as the Dulong, a transliteration of Drung.

A visit to the Putao Rawang Museum (spelled Rvwang locally) showed a migration map of its people from the northern Tibetan plateau, across the entire high country and eastward to Kham and then southward between the Mekong and Salween River, eventually crossing westward into northern Myanmar. Their language is the same as that of the Dulong of Yunnan, and has about thirty percent of words in common with that of the Nu nationality of the upper Salween valley.

While the migration of the Rawang had taken them from their historic home on a journey of thousands of kilometers, the more recent exodus of the Lisu following their missionary leaders in 1965 had taken them across from Putao to the border of India – a distance of only a couple hundred kilometers. Yet the Lisu migration was written up in contemporary times as a great religious drama.

In 1926, the Morse family left the Batang Mission in western Sichuan after five years of contract service and moved west into the upper Salween River, continuing their preaching among the Lisu and Rawang of the area as independent missionaries, working on both sides of the China/Burma border. During the War, the Morses did service for the Allies in attempting to rescue survivors of crashed planes as well as accounting for human losses and burial services for those flight pilots and crew.

I had been following much of the missionary work along the upper Mekong and Salween, including taking Swiss priest Fr Savioz back to his church in Tibet. Besides, we documented much work of the Hump pilots including creating a small theme museum. I had taken 70-year-old Dr. William Hardy back to his place of birth in Batang in 1987. He was born in 1916 in Batang, where his father, also a Dr. William Hardy, had taken over the mission clinic from Dr. Albert Shelton, who founded the Batang Mission after being inspired by Canadian missionary doctor Susie Rhjnhart's work in Tibet. In Pomona California I had met Dorothy, the daughter of Dr. Shelton.

After the Communists took hold of China in 1949, the Morse family moved further west in 1950 into northern Myanmar, finally settling in Muladi some ten kilometers south of Putao by a branch of the Malikha River. In 1965, under the military government of Ne Win, the family were given very short notice and asked to leave the country. Instead of abiding to the country's new rules, the Morses decided to head off on foot toward India, hoping to gain entry across the border and perhaps find a new settlement to continue their missionary work. Thousands of Lisu, about a quarter of the population of the Putao plain, decided to follow them, though the majority of them turned back to Putao later on. Thus the mass migration began, as portrayed in Eugene Morse's book Exodus to a Hidden Valley.

True to form of such work of religious zeal, the Lisu as well as the family members were portrayed in the book as brave, selfless and resourceful, whereas the pursuing army were timid, cowardly and clumsy. Even the Indian border officer was depicted in rather condescending fashion while the Morses were hoping for graciousness and permission to enter the country. The author described crossings of ravines and hazardous terrain, finally arriving at their new homestead settlement for the next five years. The narrative of survival against nature, though brutal are nonetheless beautiful and more palatable, including a very informative account about the native's honey collecting expeditions.

Later, the army caught up with them and sent them on a forced march to final deportation. Not surprisingly, the communists in China, which Morse had left some fifteen years before, were also featured as being godless and cold-blooded. It seems natural and obvious that the clear divide between good and bad is straightly along religious lines.

I stopped for a moment reading the book and became a bit cynical, wondering how the Morses would feel had they been born as Native Americans sent on an exodus with the calvary in hot pursuit, driven finally into the squalid paradise of latter-day Indian reservations. One of the Morses, Robert, went on to teach English at Lhasa University in the 1980s, for the cold-blooded communists! Convenience and opportunities often help people change sides in the calling of a higher cause.

For much of the ethnic region in northern Myanmar, the once largely independent Jingpo, Rawang, Lisu, Zaiwa, Lachik and Lawngwaw were suddenly enmeshed into a generalized group called the Kachin, designated as residents of a state of the same name when a new nation was born in 1947 upon exit of the British. Such high-handed geographical integration with little consideration for ethnic divides precipitated ethnic strife, which *continues to this day as insurgent struggles in this part of the country. The Kachin Independence Army (KIA) is still active after 70 years, and much feared once people leave the main roads and head into the hills.*

I visited the dilapidated church and home of the Morses in Muladi. The ruins with rusted roofs tell a tale of a church community that lasted barely 15 years before the family left the scene. The parish however continued to flourish, as most of the Lisu who departed with the Morses eventually decided to turn back. Their church was pure and pristine, like the nearby turquoise water of the upper Irrawaddy, until the year 2000 when there came a split of the group into two separate churches, one of which wanted to expand and further their work, while the other was determined to keep their parish only among the local community.

As for the Morses, today descendants of the family have started anew in Chiangmai of northern Thailand, continuing their forefather's unfinished evangelizing work, calling themselves the North Burma Christian Mission, a somewhat outdated and diehard colonialist name.

It was barely 6:30am and I am strolling the street market in heavy fog near the center of Putao. Experience tells me that once the fog lifts, the sky will be clear with the winter sun shining. Three long lines of venders are selling local vegetables, fruits, meat, smoked and freshly caught fish, and forest products like game meat and honey in bottles. A woman with a large woven basket brought out a huge native carp, perhaps five feet long, freshly caught from the nearby Malikha River, the left tributary of the upper Irrawaddy. Two hornbill heads caught my eyes, two different species.

Momentarily, a lady squatting held up in front of me a small plastic bottle with a red cap. I took a closer look — cordyceps. There was a bundle of the precious caterpillar fungus inside. Much valued for its supposed medicinal properties, this is the treasure of the high plateau that has enriched many Tibetan communities over the last few decades. Suddenly, I started seeing many more of these red cap bottles sitting at the feet of several venders.

Apparently, this is the most-prized merchandise among everything else on sale for a pittance. Sandra our Myanmar Country Manager helped me ask the price. They ranged from 5,000 Kyat (US$3.5) per piece for the golden fungus, to 2,000 Kyat for the dark black type, depending on the size and look. Small packets of three tiny pieces with a long tail and a printed description in Burmese, would sell for around 5,000 Kyat.

Collecting caterpillar fungus has become the preoccupation of the locals, and they hike for days from the plain of Putao to the high snow mountains to the north, east and west. Over the last three decades, prices have gone up thirty to fifty times depending on the grade of the harvest, thanks to an escalating demand on the Chinese side. News of such distant markets has been relayed over the high mountains of Tibet to a tiny community of some 200 Tibetans who migrated from the plateau to northern Myanmar almost a hundred years ago.

Putao Morning market / 葡萄縣晨曦市集

Market with Hornbill heads / 市集販售的犀鳥頭

Big fish from river / 河裡捕獲的大魚

Golden Cordyceps / 黃金冬蟲夏草
A second Tibetan home / 另一所藏族房子

Lady selling Cordyceps / 女子售賣冬蟲夏草

Not far from the market in Putao live around fifteen Chinese merchant families. They have been here for generations. Ms. Cun, sixty years old, was born in Putao and now runs the biggest variety store, covering merchandise from clothes, dry food, motorcycles, and farm equipment, to cement and other construction materials. She has six grown children, five of them married and living in other cities. Her two-story mansion of a house is a stone's throw away. Her father came from Heshun of Tengchong in western Yunnan. She has visited her families ancestral home five times. She should be thrilled to hear that President Xi Jinping stopped at her hometown of Heshun right after his state visit to Myanmar these past two days.

At Upper Sankhaung, a Rawang village west of Putao, a road is being built to reach the Indian border, probably someday to be connected eastward to China as part of the transport web of the Belt and Road Initiative. Here I meet 50-year-old Kyrzi. She had immigrated to Australia twelve years ago but returned to Putao for ten years to be near her mother, who is 84 years of age. Kyrzi wanted to turn her new house into a Bed & Breakfast. A clear stream flows in front of her house and she managed to install a small hydro generator for electricity, a game-changer given that the town's power is certainly uncertain. She said her father was the first Rawang pastor after the departure of the Morses.

Two of her sisters, Marta and May are also in town visiting from Yangon and Australia. May is living in Perth and married to a Chinese, a Wong like myself. Later we were to camp out at the yard of Marta, the eldest sister's home. Cold and humid with night dew, the warmth of my bivy tent attracted a slug that crawled over the tent to reach my head. In the summer monsoon season, this *would likely be a swarm of leeches instead.*

After a bowl of noodles next door to Kyrzi's home, we visited neighboring Shangkaung village. Pongbur, sixty-four-years of age, is the best-known Rawang hunter, and he has three sets of crossbow, all well used. He proudly shows me a flintlock gun he uses for hunting larger game. On the pillar of his house is a Takin trophy head. These animals, somewhat resembling mix of a cow and a goat, roam the foothills and lower slopes of the eastern Himalayas. We wanted to acquire it for display, but Pongbur brought out a much nicer specimen for us to take home.

We also procured one of his sets of crossbows with arrow pouch, poison arrows included. The tiny root he gave us is what the Rawang use to make their primitive hunting arrows lethal. We were warned to wash our hands after touching it. It took a bit of negotiation before we managed to acquire a traditional ceremonial Rawang hat. Finely woven from bamboo, it has many boar tusks attached around the rim.

A traditional blouse made from hemp became yet another prized item for our gradually growing Rawang collection. Hemp is not allowed to be grown openly since the 1970s, when the government decreed such plants may be used as drugs, not recognizing that biologically there is a different strain

Rawang hunter with takin head /
日旺獵人與羚牛牛頭

used for marijuana smoking. Drugs are indeed said to be a major problem among young people of the Putao plain, but something more potent is used, in the form of an injection.

We stayed overnight sleeping on the floor at the home of another Rawang hunter in Malikhong village to the east, by the bank of a tributary that flows into the Malikha. The next morning was Sunday and we headed to the local church before the services were to begin at 10am. The young pastor U Maritdizi was very hospitable while his wife was hurriedly making popcorn over the hearth to entertain us. At ten, Pastor M went out on the balcony and struck the bell, calling his community to service. The bell was actually a long metal gas cylinder hung on a string.

People began filing in from the village. Soon all of the church's benches were filled, with women seated to the left and men to the right. There must have been a total of 150 Christians gathered as service began with the assistant pastor, wearing a traditional Rawang coat, reading from the bible. There were plenty of young women with babies in the church, some singing from their hymn books while nursing their infants. As Pastor M was giving a long sermon, we rose to leave.

Jingpo Church / 景頗教堂

Rawang Sunday service / 日旺的主日崇拜

We had heard that nearby across the river was a Jingpo village where another church service has begun. The Jingpo are another tribe that made up the core of the KIA. Using a dug-out canoe, we paddled and poled ourselves across the shallow river and walked for ten minutes to reach Nambuyun village. We arrived barely in time to observe four Jingpo singing their hymns in chorus with a young man standing behind playing percussion guitar.

Just as they filed out of their rather spartan church, we managed to find a man living adjacent to the church to show us his watermill. His is the only one in the village, so everyone bring their grains to him for grinding. Each bushel would cost 200 Kyat for his service. The watermill, taller than a person's height in diameter, is ingeniously connected to three different machines, one for grinding rice into flour, another for husking, and a third for crushing rape seed for oil. Certainly, those of us in a modern society advocating clean energy and efficiency have something to learn here.

Besides all the cultural discovery in Putao, one highlight was a boat ride down the Malikha River. At Nutkyun village, we were told not to speak any outside languages so as to pretend to be locals. The boatman may not want to take foreigners on such a joy ride, as there are government regulations prohibiting outsiders on the river. We abided by Ram Sengh's advice and boarded a long-tail boat.

A few exciting runs through some whitewater rapids and we cruised the river with much of the pristine water glistening and reflecting from stones on the bottom. As we travelled further, the rocks on both sides were carved smooth like sculptures that made Henry Moore's creations seem rather miniscule. This was dry water season and we could imagine the vast current running through the Malikha during the monsoon season. Before we turned around, at a Buddhist pagoda set in the middle of the river, we saw many waterfowl, no doubt spending their

Multi-purpose watermill / 多功能水磨機
Kingfisher / 白喉翡翠

winter here, down from the high plateau. There were Ruddy Shelducks and cormorants, sandpipers and a few egrets. Though the locals said there were hornbills around, I did not get to see them. Just before we reached shore again, I saw a most colorful and beautiful White-breasted Kingfisher that made my day.

As my five-day sojourn to Putao was coming to an end, I thought for a moment that perhaps the missionaries had left some redeeming value behind in their trail. Almost all the Rawang, Lisu and Jingpo are now Christians, as evidenced by the many churches dotting the entire valley. As religious practitioners, they refrain from drinking and smoking. But then, when I think further, their simple living and animistic past also had few vices to begin with.

Obviously, mobile phones and the internet age, which arrived some five years ago to Putao, will initiate more dramatic changes to these people than any missionary had ever done in the past. Yet, we are all part of that current of our time, like the never-ending water of the Malikha River flowing near us, with tributaries that converge to become the mighty Irrawaddy. In the same way, all of us will soon become homogeneous in a world of the future, connected through clouds in the internet and clouds in heaven, Amen.

Sculpted rock with pagoda / 經長年雕琢的巨石與佛塔

緬北飛地

「住察瓦龍鄉的親戚邀請我們去看看。所以大概四年前，我們一行七人，在卡車和路上一路顛簸十八天，跨越六座山，才抵達這個西藏的偏遠鄉村。」哈魯是其中兩家藏族家庭的一員，目前定居於緬甸葡萄縣東部邊境的三林丹 (Sanlum Dam) 小鎮。

要爬上這條蜿蜒綿長的山路，對七十歲的哈魯來說，肯定是吃力的。這位在緬甸出生的長輩，早在一世紀前左右，父親那一代便已從察瓦龍鄉遷居到緬甸最北端，目前已有四個西藏村在此落地生根——塔溫當村、桑當村、門登村、西桃當村——共計約兩百藏民生活於此。他們聲稱自己屬多隆巴 (Drolpa) 族，歷世歷代以來，緊鄰察瓦龍而居。

「我們那一次是坐車子去昆明的，然後，我們親戚再開車把我們一路載到北京。」哈魯長期住在世界最偏遠的角落，一說起這段令他眼界大開的旅程，他炯炯有神的雙眼，在一張藏族人典型的深邃五官中，格外閃動。

他的女兒薩娜拉姆與女婿多爾吉，四年前便已搬離山區到平地去。但每年春天與夏天，女兒女婿仍會定期返回高原上。當我們在聊天時，多爾吉就在一旁忙著煮茶；他捨棄傳統的木製攪拌器，改以塑膠攪拌器來為我們準備鹹味酥油茶。

一年前，當我在緬甸南方的丹老群島跳島旅遊時，衛星電話傳來老父親跌倒入院的消

息，我必須盡速趕回香港。相隔一年，此時我已在緬甸最北端的葡萄縣，兜兜轉轉在群山圍繞的山野河谷之間，以印度為西部疆界，東至中國雲南邊境，北達西藏，繼續我的探察之旅。

伊洛瓦底江的左岸或西部支流，是流經山谷的馬里卡河。緬甸最高山是海拔五千七百四十二公尺的開加博峰 (Hkakabo Razi)，但根據最新出現於衛星定位系統的地圖標示，甘姆朗峰 (Gamlang Razi) 已遙遙領先而成最高峰。奇峰羅列的兩座山，都是喜馬拉雅東峰的一部分，水闊山高，攀山越嶺要走上好幾週。

怪石嶙峋的開加博峰，曾經難倒許多登山者，直到一九九六年，一支結合日本與西藏的登山隊伍才終於成功爬上這座桀驁難馴的高山，但後來的登山行動，卻造成兩名緬甸探險隊成員在下山時失蹤。來自懷俄明州的成員馬克‧詹金斯 (Mark Jenkins)，是我新聞工作的登山友人，為了要量測山峰高度而申請再度登山。

二戰期間，飛越「駝峰航線」的飛行員常把葡萄縣名為赫茲堡壘，一聽便知道那是當時英國殖民官取的名。這地方果然名不虛傳，其無線電台不僅為飛行員提供不可或缺的無線通訊與訊號，也引導飛機飛越險象環生的喜馬拉雅東部山脈，為戰時中國提供補給配備。這道被喻為「駱駝脊背」的駝峰航線，險阻重重，三年內超過六百台飛機因迷航而墜毀、或消失無蹤；更有報導指失

China/Myanmar aborder crossing /
中緬跨境通道
Hazardous border / 危險邊境

Dorji churning tea and wife Lamu /
多吉爾正在弄茶，旁為妻子拉姆

事的飛機數量達兩千架，無從查證。「中國探險學會」有幸保有一九四二年至四四年二戰期間，非常罕見的雙面地圖——精美印製於絲綢上的緬甸與「駝峰航線」地圖。我把地圖帶在身邊，靠它指引我方向。

日旺族的藍昇，負責我最後幾天的嚮導工作。日旺族是葡萄縣山谷區主要的族群。二十八歲的藍昇，年紀輕輕便已身經百戰，曾經長途跋涉到印緬邊境，十三天內攀登往西延伸的崇山峻嶺，為到西藏，再以六天時間往北遠征，進入雲南；然後，在八天內往東攀越六座山。他最近的探險旅程是去年十一月，為家計與謀生，而翻山越谷到獨龍江河谷。他們把麝香、冬蟲夏草、偶爾還有熊膽，賣到中國，換回時尚衣著與鞋子。雄麝香鹿腺囊中的乾燥分泌物，這樣一顆麝香囊，價格依大小不同，可以賣到五、六千人民幣。藍昇一般以達仲丹 (Dazung Dam) 鎮為出發點，那也是藍昇出生的故鄉，位處海拔一千三百公尺高地，距離葡萄縣北部大約七天的腳程。

藍昇取道進入中國的途徑，和我二零一六年的那趟行程一樣，只不過我們的方向剛好相反，我走的是四十一號界樁邊界，從中國流向緬甸的伊洛瓦底江上游流域，當地人稱之為「獨龍」(Drung)。當我們把兩國邊境的終點照片一比對，竟不謀而合，果然是同一個地點。緬甸那一邊的主要族裔稱為日旺族，其實與中國的獨龍

族是同一個族群。話說當時中國少數民族代表於五十年代齊聚北京時，與當時的領導毛主席會面。毛主席問起一位獨龍江代表的故鄉，他回答「獨龍」，自此，來自獨龍江的族群便被認定為獨龍族。

走訪葡萄縣的日旺博物館，館內展出一幅族群遷徙的地圖，可見族人從北方的西藏高原，翻過一座座峰巒疊嶂，往東前進西藏康區，輾轉南向至湄公河與薩爾溫江之間，最後再轉往西邊進入緬甸北方。日旺族的語言與雲南獨龍族幾無差異，和薩爾溫江上流河谷的怒族語言，相似度達百分之三十。

日旺族遠離故土時，踏上的是一段數千公里的迢迢遠路；相對之下，傈僳族於一九六五年追隨宣教士從葡萄縣到印度邊界的大遷徙則不算太長，全程只有數百公里。雖然如此，傈僳族離鄉背井的遷居故事，峰迴路轉，在當代歷史被記載為極富戲劇性的宗教之旅。

一九二六年，宣教士莫爾斯一家離開服務五年的四川巴塘 (Batang) 宣教會，從四川西部，轉西往薩爾溫江上游區域，以獨立宣教士身份，延續他們對傈僳族與日旺族的宣教使命，在中國與緬甸的邊境兩地，奔波往返。戰爭爆發時，莫爾斯也為同盟國服務，竭力從墜毀的飛機上搶救倖存者，尋找失蹤者，或為命喪其中的飛行官與機組人員安葬。

回想起來，我在湄公河與薩爾溫江上游與當地的宣教士事工，有過幾次接觸與印象深刻的互動。多年前，我曾護送瑞士神父沙智勇 (Savioz) 回到他西藏的教堂。此外，我們也紀錄了不少飛越「駝峰航線」的飛行員故事，並為此成立一間袖珍型主題博物館。我記得一九八七年時，我送七十歲的宣教士威廉・哈德 (William Hardy) 醫生返回他的出生地巴塘。值得一提的是，一九一六年，哈德醫生在巴塘出生，他的父親也是宣教醫師，接管了與藏族宣教緊密連結的醫療診所——這是由宣教士史

德文 (Albert Shelton) 醫師在巴塘宣教會所成立的醫療診所；而史德文則是深受加拿大傳教士蘇西‧林哈特 (Susie Rhjnhart) 醫師在西藏的工作所感召，而踏上宣教之旅。我曾在美國加州的波莫納市與史德文醫師的女兒桃樂茜 (Dorothy)，有過一面之緣。

一九四九年，共產黨執掌中國，隔年，莫爾斯舉家往西遷移至緬北，最終在葡萄縣之南，馬里卡河旁支約數十公里外的穆拉迪 (Muladi) 安頓下來。一九六五年，在當時緬甸軍事強人奈溫的政權下，莫爾斯在極短時限內被勒令出境。放棄對新政權法令的順從，莫爾斯決定再度拔營離開，轉移陣地，徒步前往印度，心想或可跨越邊境，找到新據點、新族群，繼續他們的傳教工作。上千名傈僳族人決定跟隨莫爾斯，離鄉遷移至他處；雖然後來大多又選擇回流歸巢，但第一時間離開的人數眾多，幾乎佔了整個葡萄縣四分之一人口。於是，族人攜家帶眷，追隨領袖，展開聲勢浩大的長途遷徙之旅；此事件後來被記錄於莫爾斯著作《出緬甸入隱秘谷》(Exodus to a Hidden Valley) 書中。

一如既往的認知，類似天賦使命離不開根深蒂固的宗教熱誠，傈僳族與莫爾斯家庭在書中被形塑成勇敢、無私與足智多謀的形象，而追趕他們的士兵則表現得膽怯懦弱、笨拙粗糙。面對莫爾斯家族懇切要求進入印度境內時，顧守邊境的印度海關人員也在書中被描繪成不可一世的高姿態。作者詳述長途跋涉的遷移旅程中，眾人如何跨越溝壑，泥船渡河般步步為營，最終抵達新據點，在那裡住了五年。為了活命與生存，這群人想方設法與大自然搏鬥，過程雖然艱辛，但也飽含生命之美，其中包括採集野生蜂蜜的詳盡資訊記載。

後來，掌權者的士兵追到叢林裡驅趕，強迫他們行軍，遣送出境。莫爾斯曾經揮別

十五年的中國共產黨，自然也被敘述為邪惡與冷血無情的政權。我其實並不感意外，因為宗教擅於二分法，聖俗、善惡，似乎只有一條非黑即白的界線，是非分明。

我掩卷沉思，心中衍生一些質疑與批判——我好奇，如果莫爾斯生來是美國原住民，歷經窮追猛打之苦，而最終被趕盡殺絕到貧瘠艱困之地，一個後來被稱之為印第安保護區的地方，不曉得換位思考時，莫爾斯對此議題將作何感想？莫爾斯第二代家族的成員羅伯（Robert），在八十年代成為西藏拉薩大學的英文老師，誰能料到多年後，他竟為當初那個「冷血無情」的共產黨服務！或許，被更崇高的理想感召，的確有助人們見機行事，改變立場。

對大部分緬北的族群區域或部落，原來各自獨立的族群——景頗族、日旺族、傈僳族、載瓦族、勒期族與浪峨族，一夜之間被結合歸類為一大族系，統稱「克欽族」(Kachin)；而一九四七年當英殖民離開緬甸時，一個名稱一樣的新省度，就這麼順理成章地出現——「克欽邦」。以如此高壓手段來進行區域整併，對民族之間的分化問題欠缺周詳顧慮，使克欽邦陷落種族衝突的紛擾，其中錯綜複

Old House of the Morses / 莫爾斯的老房子　　　　Abandoned church at Muladi / 位於穆拉迪的荒廢教堂

雜的糾結與叛亂分子動輒激戰的不安局勢，延續至今。七十年已過，克欽獨立軍 (KIA) 至今仍「戰鬥力」不減；因此，出入此區的人一旦從主要幹道轉入山區時，最怕遇見這群驍勇善戰之士。

我走訪了莫爾斯一家在穆拉迪的據點——殘破不堪的教堂和住家。眼前破敗的廢墟與腐朽的屋瓦，訴說一段建造了十五年的教會社群生活，直到他們離開。莫爾斯一家雖已離去，但曾經跟著莫爾斯遷移的大部分傈僳人，最終決定返回故里，所以這教區持續開花結果。傈僳人的教堂素雅樸質，一如鄰近的伊洛瓦底江上游的清新水流。但 2000 年一場傳教理念分歧導致教區分裂，原有的靜美與和諧，開始出現裂痕，一分為二：一方主張往外拓展開發，另一方則執意留守當地教區，深耕不動。

至於莫爾斯家族，其後代子孫已在各地展開新生活，有的在泰北清邁傳教，繼承祖先未竟的宣教使命，將他們的傳教工作定調為「緬北基督宣教會」(North Burma Christian Mission)，聽起來有些不合時宜，添加了幾分狂熱殖民主義的色彩。

近清晨六點半，我在濃霧中散步到葡萄縣的早市。經驗告訴我，晨霧一旦散去，撥雲見日的天空必然澄澈燦亮。排列成三行的路邊攤販，售賣當地蔬菜、水果、肉類、煙燻與剛捕撈的鮮魚，還有一些產自深山的野味與瓶裝野蜜。一名婦女從編織籃中取出一隻肥大生猛的當地鯉魚，魚身約有五尺長，剛剛才從附近伊洛瓦底江上流旁支馬里卡河中捕獲的「現撈魚」。不過，最吸引我目光的，是旁邊兩隻不同品種的犀鳥頭。

還來不及回過神來，一名蹲在路邊的女子，把手上一個栓緊紅色瓶蓋的小塑膠瓶，在

我面前舉起來。我趨前定睛一看，是冬蟲夏草。瓶子裡裝了一群珍貴的真菌類蛹蟲；這些蛹蟲不僅藥用價值高，且是高原上的寶藏，更是藏民過去數十年的主要經濟作物。頃刻間，越來越多紅色瓶蓋的瓶子紛紛出現眼前，它們被置放於一些攤販的腳前。

顯然這是所有利潤微薄的產品中，最價格不菲的東西。我請隨行的我們學會緬甸經理珊卓拉代我詢問價格。一般而言，蛹蟲大小與長相為定價標準，黃金真菌蛹蟲每條從五千緬元（約折合三點五美元）起跳，而黑真菌蛹蟲的價格則為每條兩千緬元。另外內含三條長尾小蛹蟲的小包裝，包裝袋上印製了緬文說明，則要價五千緬元。

Kyrzi at her new home / 齊爾姿於她的新家

採收冬蟲夏草已成為當地居民最首要的工作，他們為此而從葡萄縣的平地，跋山涉水，迎風冒雪地往北、往東又往西，到積雪高峰去。過去三十多年來，隨著採收等級與中國市場日益高漲的需求，冬蟲夏草的價格大幅成長了三十至五十倍之多。這些遙遠市場的行情與消息，有賴兩組西藏社群輪番傳遞——其中一組是居住高山地帶的藏民，另外則是百多年前從高原遷移至緬北，為數約兩百位藏民的小群體。

距離葡萄縣當地市場不遠處，聚集了十五個華裔商人的社群。他們已好幾代定居於此。六十歲的陳太太在葡萄縣出生，經營一間當地規模最大的百貨商店，產品種類繁多，衣食住行全都包——服裝、乾糧、機車、農具器材、水泥與其他建築材料。陳太太的六名孩子都已成年，其中五人已婚，定居於其他城鎮。她那兩層樓的別墅大宅就在店鋪附近。陳太太的父親來自雲南西部中緬邊境，騰沖市的和順鎮，她已先後返鄉探親五次了。如果她知道中國領導習近平兩天前訪視緬甸後，曾短暫停留她父親的老家和順，或許會讓她激動萬分。

在葡萄縣西邊的日旺族村落附近，鋪設了一道通往印度邊界的馬路，或許有一天會銜接至中國東邊，建構起「一帶一路」的交通網。我在當地認識了五十歲的齊爾姿。她在十二年前移民至澳洲，但後來為了陪伴老母親而返回葡萄縣，母親今年八十四歲，齊爾姿已在家鄉待了十年。一道清澈小溪流經她家門前，齊爾姿最近想把新房子整修成民宿，這位想要改變遊戲規則的女子，先動手安裝了一台小型水電發電機，由此可見小鎮的電力供應並不穩定。齊爾姿告訴我，自從宣教士家庭莫爾斯離開之後，她的父親接任傳教之託，成為日旺族的首位牧師。

齊爾姿的兩位姐妹瑪妲與梅，這段期間剛好分別從仰光與澳洲前來探親。梅在澳洲伯斯 (Perth) 定居，嫁給當地一位和我同姓的華人。不久，我們齊聚於大姐馬坦家的草地上露營。夜空下的冷空氣與濕氣，伴隨露水，更顯濕寒，而我溫暖的帳篷引來一隻取暖的蚰蜒，攀越帳篷而停留在我頭上。如果這是夏天的雨季，爬上身的恐怕不是蚰蜒，而是一群蜂擁而至的水蛭了。

在齊爾姿家隔壁吃了一碗麵，我們起身走訪鄰近的尚光 (Shangkaung) 村。六十四歲的村民彭布，是日旺族家喻戶曉的獵人；家中備有三套常用的弩弓。他難掩驕傲神色，向我們展示了用來獵捕大型動物的燧發槍。房子樑柱上高掛羚牛牛頭，那是他狩獵的戰利品。這些羚牛類似牛與羊的複合體，喜馬拉雅山脈東邊的山麓丘陵與較低的斜坡上，經常可見牠們的蹤跡。我們表達購買意願，想要以此作展示之用，彭布卻取出另一個更完整的標本讓我們帶回去。

我們也想向他購買一套附有箭靶袋的弩弓，包括一些毒箭。他把一支不起眼的細小根莖交給我，那是日旺族用來製作致命毒箭的

Huruq's high country products / 哈魯的高原產物
Marta and May at mother's home / 瑪妲與梅於母親的家
CERS acquisitions / 中國探險學會的收穫

材料。他警告我們一旦觸碰過這些東西，都要洗手。此外，我們看上了日旺族在傳統祭典時戴在頭上的帽子，為此和主人稍微協商了一會兒才如願以償。這帽子以竹片編織，同時把野豬獠牙也附著帽沿上。

一件傳統大麻材質的女上衣，成了我們另一個想像中的目標物，希望為袋子裡逐漸增多的日旺蒐藏品，再追加一項。自一九七零年代開始，政府已嚴禁公然種植大麻，以免大麻被濫用而成毒品原料，但其實就植物原理來看，吸大麻的毒品屬另一品種，兩「麻」大不同。提起毒品，那確實是葡萄縣年輕人最大的問題，但更棘手的是從吸食到注射的使用方式，令人非常憂心。

沿著馬里卡河的支流岸邊前進，我們在馬里康 (Malikhong) 村往東之處，認識了另一位日旺族獵人，並在他家打地鋪過夜。隔天是禮拜天，我們前往當地一間教會，趕在十點前參加主日禮拜。年輕牧師馬立迪茲熱情好客，他太太則在爐灶邊忙著煮玉米花來招待我們。十點準時，馬牧師走到陽台外敲鐘，提醒社區居民，聚會時間到了。那鐘其實是一個長條金屬瓦斯氣缸瓶，掛在繩索上，便成了鐘。

村民陸陸續續從四方匯聚。不一會兒，教堂裡的長椅上都坐滿人了，男女有別，女士靠左邊坐，男士的座位則靠右。放眼望去，至少有一百五十名會友齊聚參加崇拜。一開始時，身穿日旺傳統外套的助理牧師上台朗讀一段聖經經文。席間有好多年輕媽媽手上抱著嬰兒一起來，有些還一邊吟唱詩歌一邊親餵寶寶。馬牧師開始長篇大論講道時，我們便悄然離席了。

我們聽說河對岸的景頗 (Jingpo) 村也有一間教堂，他們的主日崇拜才剛開始。克欽獨立軍的核心成員中，有不少是景頗族裔。坐上獨木舟，我們在水淺的溪流上划槳而過，再步行十分鐘抵達南布勻 (Nambuyun) 村。我們一到，正好聽到四個景頗人的聖詩合唱，其中有個年輕人站在合唱隊後方彈奏吉他。

聖歌隊成員離開簡陋小教堂時，我們也藉機認識了一名住教會旁邊的先生。他向我們展示他的水磨機。全村只有他有水磨機，所以，每一家的穀物都得送來研磨。每一蒲式耳 (約 36.37 公升) 的研磨費是兩百緬元。這台水磨機的直徑，高過一個成年人的平均身高，設計精密，與三個不同的機械緊密連結，一台將大米磨成粉，一台脫殼去穀，第三台機器則把種籽壓榨成油。我們這些經常把乾淨能源與高效率掛嘴邊的現代社會人，這裡的另類生活值得我們來此學學。

在葡萄縣的文化新發現，收穫滿滿，而另一個精彩重點是搭船至馬里卡河的旅程。我們在納特昆 (Nutkyun) 村時，有人提醒我們閉口不言，偽裝成當地人。當地政府明文禁止外地人乘船過河，所以，船夫若知道我們的真實身份，肯定不願載我們這群外國人遊船兜風。我們別無他法，只能乖乖就範，順從嚮導藍昇的警戒，搭上一艘長尾船。

幾次穿越浪頭激流的水上，刺激又好玩，河流清澈，水底碎石反射的閃閃光點，映照於波光粼粼的水面。再往前去，河岸兩邊的巨石被水流削磨得無比光滑，仿若鬼斧神工的雕塑，相比之下，雕塑家亨利・摩爾 (Henry Moore) 的偉大作品也顯得小巫見大巫了。當時是大旱水乾的季節，不難想象雨季期間的馬里卡河，是如何水高浪急了。回頭前，我們發現一座佛塔就這樣聳立於河床之間，一旁還有不少水禽遊走覓食，想必是從高原處來此避寒過冬。我們還看到赤麻鴨、鸕鷀、磯鷸和幾隻白鷺。雖然當地人告訴我們周遭有犀鳥，但我始終沒看到。回到岸邊前，一隻色彩斑駁的白喉翡翠，

竟出現眼前，能親眼目睹這迷人的美麗身影，令我樂不可支。

我的葡萄縣五天行程，接近尾聲。離開前，我沉思良久，心想或許早期那些披荊斬棘的宣教士，確實為族人留下珍貴的救贖價值。今天，幾乎所有日旺族、傈僳族與景頗族都是基督徒，滿山滿谷林立的教堂是最佳明證。為了實踐信仰，他們不菸不酒；不過，再深入思索，這群人一直以來就過慣了簡樸生活，加上他們根深蒂固的泛靈論背景，本來就累積不了太多生活惡習。

只是，普遍的手機與網路時代，早已在五年前，便已鋪天蓋地席捲葡萄縣，想必對當地居民帶來更驚人的衝擊，甚至遠比過去宣教士留下的影響還要強大深遠。然而，我們都是這波現代潮流的一份子，一如附近那條川流不息的馬里卡河，聚合多少旁支溪流，最終，匯入源遠流長的伊洛瓦底江。同理，我們雖然來自不同族群，但其中的差異性隨即將被抹平——百川歸海，殊途同歸——最終成為世界大家庭的一員，把我們從網路的雲端與天堂的雲彩中，相連起來！阿們。

Kid's rafting near Muladi / 孩子在穆拉迪附近泛舟
Rock art / 石頭藝術

珍稀之書

RAREST AMONG BOOKS

Hong Kong - March 8, 2020

RAREST AMONG BOOKS
20 copies made circa 1934

"Go ahead take it home with you," offered Captain Moon Chin casually. "Huh, are you sure?" I asked in return. "Why not, I'm turning 106 in a few months," Moon added. Anyone would understand the high value of such a book, but few would appreciate it as much as I do. Now the burden is on me to become a good custodian of this extremely rare book, leather bound and with a name inscribed in gold on its cover.

This is not the first time Moon has given me something so valuable. Many years ago, he handed me a Dunhuang mural piece that was exchanged in 1946 for sale of his downstairs home with a garden in the French Concession area of Shanghai. At that time, he had just founded his first airline, Central Air Transport Corp (CATC), and bought one of the corner villas from Mayor Wu Tieh-cheng in the tony district on Kang Ping Road for 185 gold bars.

But for me, the most valuable gift has been our friendship, and the wonderful stories that he has recounted to me over the almost two decades that we have known each other. I visit Moon at least twice a year, staying at his home in San Francisco for a night or two. If I am pressed for time, I still make a day trip to spend time with him.

Book given to Huang Kiang Chuan /
送給 Huang Kiang Chuan 的書

Still, this book is precious. The name inscribed on the cover is Huang Kiang Chuan. At the time the book was produced, in 1934, only twenty copies were made, each with actual black & white prints meticulously set on pages with wax paper between, like an album. The one I received is labelled Number 11, handwritten on a space left for that purpose. Huang was the Chairman of China National Aviation Corp (CNAC), put in place by the Nationalist government for a joint venture with Pan American Airways. China's government at the time held a 55% share, whereas Pan Am had 45%.

Since 1931, Moon had been a pilot and had quickly become the most experienced Chinese pilot for CNAC, flying until the end of the Second World War when he founded his own airline. During the latter part of the War, Moon pioneered the first flight across the Karakorum to open the western Hump route. It was a precaution in case the Japanese would take all of Burma, thus closing the Hump of the eastern Himalayas,the life-line to supply the Chinese forces resisting the Japanese advance. Later in 1951, he was to found another airline, Foshing Airlines in Taiwan. It seems natural that this book would be passed down from CNAC's Chairman to the Chinese Chief Pilot. But from Moon to me, it is strictly through trust and friendship.

The short introductory note that precedes the prints is titled "The Mail Must Go". Some of us may be familiar with the Disney song with a similar title, about how, against all odds, the mail must go through. Whereas this book was compiled through the courtesy and from the pictures of Mr. A.M. Chapelain, a Frenchman who served as China's Postal Commissioner in Shanghai over a period of three decades, from the late Qing Dynasty to the early Chinese Republic era.

The two-page eight paragraph description is so poetic, romantic and descriptive that quoting from it would not do it justice. Thus, it is reproduced below as it appears in the book:

"High up in the mountains where the headwaters of the Yangtze lie. The packed snows thaw slowly in a warming spring sun. The waters begin to flow...slowly at first, then more and more swiftly. They tumble, swirl and froth, and on reaching the narrow gorges, they become a mighty river.

Hubei: Post boat being pulled up
the rapids of the Yangtze /
湖北：郵船在長江急湍中拉縴的情況

Guizhou: Caravan of heavy mail couriers /
貴州：遞送重量郵件的郵遞隊伍

Henan: Courier passing Lung Men Temple /
河南：郵遞員途經龍門廟

Tumultuous, whitecapped, roaring and echoing up the towering mountain sides, obliterating all other sound.

Against this inferno of water a junk moves upstream. From her prow the tow ropes stretch, taut as over lines, to curl around the shoulders and bodies of her trackers trudging the narrow tow path. Foot by foot they fight their way forward. Hour after hour, undaunted, these hardy men toil on, till the great rapids are passed and another battle is won for transportation.

In the great wastes of China's farthest hinterland, plain and desert and rock – strewn foothills stretch out, far as the eye can reach, hot and brilliant in the summer sun. Miles of wilderness lie between hamlet and village and towns. Between them are no roads, only a footpath winding its tortuous way where the going seems least difficult.

Along this path a man moves at a brisk jogtrot alone in all the vast terrain. Balanced on his shoulder is a pole, from either end of which are suspended bags of mail. He is one of the fast couriers of the Chinese Post Office, one of the thousands of men to whose courage, stamina and faithfulness are entrusted the mails along China's 250,000 miles of overland fast courier service.

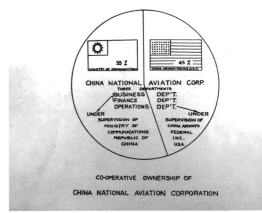

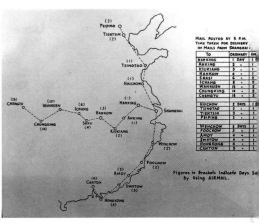

Ownership of CNAC / 中國航空公司的擁有權
Days and time saved by air /
飛行省回來的日數與時間

Jiangsu: Inland heavy mail courier /
江蘇：遞送重量郵包的郵遞員

He has come twenty miles. He has another twenty miles to go before his day is done...before he turns his trust over to the next runner, who jogtrots on through the night. Forests, uplands and wilderness, the autumn night merges them into a blur of blackness. Only the mountains are half distinct as they bulk against the sky; across the landscape, a tiny glow of light bobs along unflagging, purposeful, it is the lantern that the courier carries to light his footsteps through the night. He carries a spear, too, protection against wolves, whose howling he can hear in the dark.

Oftentimes, it is "bandit – country he must traverse. Always he does so in safety, for even the bandit respects the courier's uniform; on and on he goes, jogtrotting his forty miles, carrying now light-mail, now heavy, precious cargo that must be delivered.

Then winter comes, with its biting winds and blinding snowstorms. Over the bleak country side, here snow covered and there frozen hard, the runners continue endlessly to ply their routes; not only foot-couriers, but mounted couriers, buffalo carts, mule and camel packs, railroads, steamboats... A vast organization criss-crossing the country with a galvanic net of transportation.

The dash from marathon, the message to Garcia, the pony express...

Brilliant feats though they are in man's endless striving for swift communication...cannot compare with the panorama of China's sustained and magnificent efforts... Efforts that remain unrelaxed, day and night, through all the changing seasons, the entire year round."

Romanticism aside, we select below a number of the most dramatic pictures depicting the ground mail service and how China transitioned into the early air mail age, when passenger traffic was considered low priority, subject-to-load only after mail cargo. While it allows us to enjoy a glimpse into the past, we should also remember and appreciate the hardships of older generations. It is through their ingenuity and perseverance that this new generation can start life from a much higher platform. For young adults today, please take stock and have higher expectations of yourself, rather than discarding the older generations into the dustbins of history.

Henan: Hauling a fast courier over a city wall /
河南：快遞郵遞員以繩攀越城牆

Shanxi: Light mail courier near twin pagodas /
山西：遞送輕量郵件的郵遞員，途經雙塔附近

珍稀之書 一九三四年的二十本限量發行

「你就把它帶回去吧。」陳文寬機長一派輕鬆地提議。「啊，你確定嗎？」我不可置信地回答。他補充回應道：「有何不可？我再過幾個月就一百零六歲啦。」

任誰都曉得我手上這本書是無價之寶，但不多人如我般懂得欣賞珍視，愛不釋手。這本超極罕見的書，以皮革包裝，封面以燙金字刻印；而今，保管連城之璧的重責大任，已轉移到我身上，我得成為好管家。

事實上，陳文寬不是第一次把貴重東西送我。多年前，他曾把一幅敦煌飛天壁畫交給我，那是他在一九四六年出售位於上海法租界的一樓花園洋房後，以此代價換來的壁畫。當時，他首次創立中央航空公司 (CATC)，以一百八十五塊金條，從時任上海市長的吳鐵城手中購入位於康平路一間角落別墅。

但對我而言，更彌足珍貴的其實是我們之間的友情，以及將近二十年來，這段相濡以沫的所有美好故事。我每年至少都會去探望他兩次，到他舊金山的家住一兩晚。如果時間倉促，我仍會當天來回去看看他、陪陪他。

當然，這本書無比珍貴。書封面刻寫著 *Huang Kiang Chuan* 這個英文名字。書籍出版

於一九三四年，只印了二十本，每一頁都是白紙黑字、精美排版、以蠟紙相間，仿若畫冊般精緻。我拿到的那一本，空白處標示了手寫的數字「11」。黃先生是當時「中國航空公司」(China National Aviation Corp.) 的董事長；這家當年由國民政府與泛美航空合資成立的航空公司，中國政府握有百分之五十五股權，而泛美航空的股份則是百分之四十五。

自一九三一年起，陳文寬短時間內便從飛機師一躍而升為全中國最身經百戰的中航機長，在成立自己的航空公司之前，他一直堅守飛行崗位直到二戰期間。二戰末期，陳文寬被委以重任，負責飛越「喀喇崑崙山脈」之首航，開啟向西的駝峰航線。那是一趟預防性的飛行計劃，以阻止日軍一旦取下緬甸後，把喜馬拉雅東邊山脈的駝峰航線封鎖而斷絕中國的補給線。一九五一年，陳文寬再創另一家航空公司：台灣的復興航空。照理來說，這本書合理應該從中航董事長傳承給機長；但陳文寬把它交給我，純粹出於我們之間的信任與友情。

書中簡短的序言有個標題，上面寫著「信件必需送達」(The Mail Must Go)。這或許會令你想起標題類似、耳熟能詳的迪士尼兒歌，提及無論途經多少挑戰與困難，寄出去的信件必定送達收件人手中。但這本珍稀之書，其實要感激法籍人士乍配林 (A.M. Chapelain) 慨然提供重要影像與照片才得以如願；乍配林從清末到

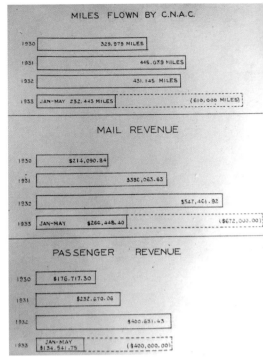

Miles flown and revenues of CNAC /
中國航空公司的飛行里數與營運收入

民國初年曾擔任上海郵政管理局局長逾三十年。

書中那兩頁八段的敘述，詩意與浪漫之情躍然紙上，若想引用其中內容來加以詮釋，恐怕掛一漏萬，難以完整表達。於是，我乾脆把書中內文複述如下：

「巍然屹立的山嶺，那裡是長江上游的源頭。團團冰雪在春日暖照下，逐漸融化。水開始流動……起初是涓涓細流，然後暢流而下。那些水一下滔滔汩汩，傾瀉奔流而濺出水花，流動至峽谷灣處，頃刻間便化為泱泱大河。水流激盪而濤涌波裏，那氣壯山河之態勢，在高深莫測的山間像鼓樂齊鳴，把其他聲音都壓下了。」

「翻江倒海之中，一艘帆船逆流而上。纜繩牢牢拖拉著船首，層層堆疊地綁緊，纏繞船身的肩膀與身子，導引她隨風轉舵，竭力通過那狹窄的水域。縴夫們咬緊牙根，拉縴引帆向，迂迴前進。一小時復一小時，這群壯漢不屈不撓，力爭上游，直至乘風破浪，順風而行；又戰勝了一場水路運輸的硬仗。」

Henan: Heavy mail on wheel-barrows drawn by mule and donkeys /
河南：裝載重量郵件之小車以人力和驢子拖拉

Chih Li: Cart service transporting heavy mail /
直隸：轉運重量郵件的車運服務

「在中國最遙遠的蠻荒之地，那些平原、荒漠與石塊鋪成的山麓丘陵，綿延伸展至眼目所及之處，在炎炎夏日下，熾烈而刺眼。千里荒原隱身坐落於村落、小鎮與城市之間，但連結目的地之間，卻無路可循；在蜿蜒曲折的道路上，披荊斬棘，只能仰賴依稀可辨的零星足跡，難行且行。」

「有人一路在無邊無際的貧瘠之地上，步履輕快地獨自奔走。他肩膀上掛著一根平衡身子的竿子，竿子兩端各垂掛郵包。在中國郵政局裡上千名郵遞員中，他是動作最快的員工之一。那裡的郵遞員各個勇氣十足，孜孜不輟，而且盡忠職守，在中國二十五萬里的廣袤大地上，他們受託帶著郵件東奔西跑，浪跡天涯，提供最快的郵遞服務。」

「他走了二十里路。前頭還有二十里路，然後，一天的任務才結束……但在此之前，他得先將未竟之業——負責跑夜路之重責大任，託付承接下一棒的夥伴。深秋的夜晚將黝黯沉寂的密林、高原與曠野，都吞噬在一片天昏地黑之中。唯有遠方的山峰，高聳

Chih Li: Heavy mail transported by camels between Kalgan and Urga /
直隸：駱駝載運重量郵件由張家口至庫倫
Sichuan: Heavy mail by foot courier from Chongqing to Chengdu /
四川：重量郵件由郵遞員徒步從重慶送至成都
Chih Li: Mounted postman delivering mail at Beidaihe /
直隸：北戴河騎驢子送件的郵遞員

Stinson plane used on the Shanghai-Beijing route /
航行於上海、北京路線的司汀遜式飛機
Loening amphibian used on Yangtze river line /
航行於長江線的洛寗式水陸兩用飛機

1921: First airplane to carry mail in China between Beijing and Jinan /
1921 年中國首次航空郵運，送遞於北京與濟南之間

Henan: Tung Kwan Ting to Kwan Yin Tang fast
courier fonding a stream /
河南：幢關廳至觀音堂間快遞郵遞員涉水遞送

「入雲，觸及天空而隱隱然澄澈透亮。跋山涉水之間，忽明忽暗的微弱燈源，穩穩地探照，那是郵遞員隨身提著的燈籠，要把緊湊的步伐照亮，才能摸黑前進。夜半三更，隱約聽見狼嗥狗叫，不怕，他身上也戴著長矛，隨時保護自己免受野狼攻擊。」

「有些時候，豺狼當道時，他還必須來回冒險於那些土匪惡徒出入之地。大部分時候，他會謹慎處理，以安全為重，因為一般匪徒也會因他那身郵遞員的制服而敬他三分；就這樣，他一路再闖蕩奔走四十里路，身上承載了輕重緩急的郵件——那些——必寄出、必需送達的重要郵件。」

「冬天來了，冷冽刺骨的寒風與難以抵禦的暴雪，也隨之而來。在人跡罕至的窮鄉僻壤，白雪覆蓋，天寒地凍而寸步難行，但那提著郵件的跑者仍步履堅定，走他的路；除了步行送信的郵遞員，還有翻山越嶺的、牛車送件的；還有騾隊與駱駝群的馱包運送、鐵路與水路的郵務……。一個龐大的組織，想方設法串聯起四通八達的交通網絡，縱橫交錯，不遠千里。」

「馬拉松長跑後的短程衝刺，把信送給加西亞，小馬快遞……就算他們已竭智盡力，儘管他們馬不停蹄地追求更快速的郵務傳送……卻仍追趕不上中國那拔山超海的雄偉氣勢與努力……無論日夜、無論四季，從歲首至年終，都鍥而不捨地，全力以赴。」

撇開浪漫主義不談，我們精挑細選了幾張最具戲劇張力的圖片，描繪中國初期的陸路郵務如何轉型至航空郵務的過程。當時的客運相較於郵務貨運，僅屬稍為次要的業務，只能在有剩餘重量空檔的情況下才能載客。這些實況重現，讓我們可以一窺那些陳年往事，藉此讓我們謹記上一代的艱困，也對他們的努力表達敬意。有他們的智慧才智與堅持不懈，新的一代才可能在更高的平台上，開展新的生活。而對今天的年輕族群而言，請自我檢視與衡量，建立更高的自我期許，而非擅自把老一輩的信念丟到歷史洪流中，棄之不顧。

Fujian: Rural post collector on his round / 福建：鄉村收信員的常務

中國探險學會的
客席藝術家與經紀項目

CERS ARTIST RESIDENCY AND AGENCY

Hong Kong – March 9, 2020

Hong Kong – March 9, 2020

CERS ARTIST RESIDENCY AND AGENCY
A new model in supporting and representing artists

"I appreciate art, but I do not appreciate artists," I said bluntly to the impassive face of Zwe. He looked back at me blandly as if I was talking to a wall. I double-majored in Journalism and Art in college, and know well how artists are, or pretend to be. For me, I have my left brain to supplement the right. The better the artist, the more right-brain leaning he or she is, and the harder to manage her or him, if even at all possible.

I elaborated on decades of knowing artists with right brain in surplus, and left brain in deficit. In the early 1980s, through the University of Southern California where I worked, I even brought two Chinese artists to the US, resulting in their success and ultimate immigration into the country.

Zwe and a woman artist Phyu have been taking up my former residence on the hill here in Zhongdian. The wooden building is a three-story villa looking down on pine forest and fish ponds, the scene descending beyond to an ensemble of buildings, pavilions and kiosks, including a writer/ composer residence, a multi-function main premises and a museum. Altogether eleven buildings make up the CERS Zhongdian Center on the outskirt of what today is known as Shangri-la. I have moved down to a small one-room abode which still provides enough sanctuary, but spares me from the ups and downs on the hill several times a day just for meals or meeting visitors.

Speaking to Zwe, I hesitated and held back on the specifics of why I was a bit upset. I am not a drinker, but in the kitchen of the villa, I kept a fine selection of liquor; whisky, brandy, wine and Chinese fuel-grade white lightning, intended for visiting friends. They've been on the kitchen counter for almost two decades. When I checked, they were all empty, the contents gone. Zwe is known to be a good drinker, or a good drunk. But Zwe is also one hell of an artist that I would like to try to represent, and we are hosting him as our first-ever CERS artist in residence.

Sandra, our Myanmar Country Manager, first approached him in Yangon, after I bought one of his paintings at Inle Lake. Zwe asked whether he could bring his sister who, he said, is also an artist. I said no problem, bring her along. Sister she wasn't. Phyu turned out to be a skillful painter in her own right, a friend of Zwe, who is forever

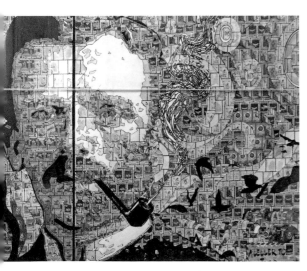

Zwe's Vincent & Theo painting / 茲易的文森與西奧畫作

Phyu's biker in rain / 傅宇的雨中騎車者

Zwe on HM Explorer /
茲易於探險船「HM 探險家號」
Zwe at CERS house / 茲易於中國探險學會的新家

catering to him. Zwe was made an orphan when both of his parents passed away after he ran away to art school in Yangon. His home was in Rakhine State, now made notorious for the expulsion, or some say voluntary exodus, of the Rohingya people, and continued fighting between the army and local ethnic militias.

Zwe's family was poor and could not support him through art school. He was known to share leftover lunch from fellow classmates, and went hungry during the weekends when everyone else went home. It thus may have provided fodder for his developing into someone who is used to pilfering, a skillful scavenger. His chain-smoking habit also led to health problems, which has curtailed somewhat his active painting.

Zwe is known for using stamps or old withdrawn paper money to create his paintings. His earlier works, painting on canvas, are all inspired by social ills and injustice in his country, thus resulting in the somewhat progressive to radical themes of his paintings. However, it is not easy to find a ready buyer for such works of art. Luckily for CERS, the difficulties of this first attempt to host artists in residence was not too hard to surmount, despite their eating and sleeping at totally undefined odd hours. Later on, we were to host the two artists on our exploration boat in Myanmar, as well as at our premises at Inle Lake. Phyu, as fortune would have it, turned out *to be quite a talented artist as well. Her paintings of children are a joy to see, and her water-marked paintings occasionally have surprises hidden to be discovered gradually.*

What came as another nice surprise was Phyu's family. Her father and his three daughters are all artists. I visited her at her most humble home on a back street in Monywa, a city some two hours west of Mandalay. Seeing her tiny bedroom where she painted by squatting on her bed with a canvas propped next to it was not a surprise. Nor was meeting her sister Swe Zin Latt, who is now teaching sculpture at Mandalay University. All along, I assumed the three siblings must have gotten into art after being influenced by their father. Not so.

Phyu's portrait painting / 傅宇的人像畫作

Young Aung San Suu Kyi / 年輕的翁山蘇姬

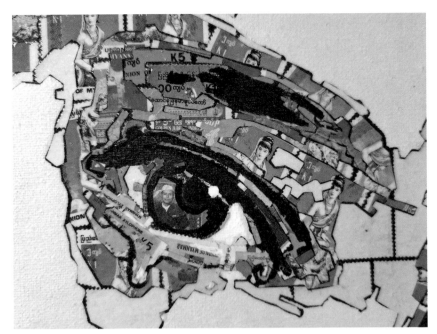

Iris with Gen. Aung San stamp / 以翁山將軍郵票拼貼成的瞳孔
Detail of lips with stamps / 以郵票拼貼成的嘴唇細部

U Soe Tint the father had always wanted to become an artist. But such a vocation could hardly provide for the upbringing of three children. So, U Soe Tint maintained a regular job until the three girls were grown and had established themselves as working artists. Only then did their father, in turn, become an artist, the last in the family, now making sculptures using natural gemstones.

However, not all artists are as dedicated as Phyu's family. I have collected three pieces of Kyaw Zay Yar's paintings, admiring the surrealistic style of his landscapes, especially the way he exaggerated figures of Buddhist monks, which he himself once was. He also occasionally applies gold leaf into his art, reminiscent of early Buddhist mural art. By the time I took an interest to inviting him as our resident artist, he had not painted for four years, with his family keeping him indoors. He had succumbed to the intensity of drugs, being surreally hooked on to something that probably resulted in his somewhat psychedelic works of art. I decided to buy his last three remaining pieces for our collection.

As for CERS, our new experimental model was inspired by the spirit of exploration, providing support to artists in countries where CERS has projects and operations. A small and select list of emerging individual artists will be invited to stay and work as resident artists at CERS premises in China, Myanmar, the Philippines and Hong Kong.

These artists can produce their art in diverse media with results being exposed, and offered for sale, to seletive and discriminating CERS supporters. CERS will repatriate the regular agent's proceeds to the artist's home country to support non-profit conservation work. Pieces sold to CERS friends will generally be made available to the artists for future exhibition as well.

Given that CERS has multiple facilities in serene locations, we have begun using these premises, when not fully utilized, to accommodate writers and composers. In 2019 we started a pilot program of invited resident artists, two at a time, beginning with the two visiting artists from Myanmar.

This program will in time include artists from Bhutan, the Philippines, Lao PDR and other neighboring countries where CERS expects to have a long-term presence. Ultimately this format would also allow artists from different emerging countries of Asia to interact with each other. Our focus will be on emerging artists little-known except in their native land, yet with artistic skills and interpretation that can be appreciated by a larger circle of art lovers, be they collectors or exhibition visitors.

We do not expect to represent such artists for a long period of time, but to be the catalyst to make their work known to a wider public. For our next round, I've been checking on artists from Bhutan. Further down the road, I also hope to include more primitive types of art, created by shaman or other members of the three-hundred strong Batak tribe whom we are now working with in the jungles of Palawan in the southern Philippines.

The Batak are also heavy drinkers, but it would not be my wine they consume. Their alcoholic beverage is not from bottle but from nature, fermented liquor produced directly from, and on the top of, the coconut palm. Of those we have plenty, as our Palawan site hosts over one thousand coconut palms!

中國探險學會的
客席藝術家與經紀項目
支持與舉薦藝術家的新模式

「我欣賞藝術,但不欣賞藝術家。」面對茲易表情木然的臉,我直言不諱。他看著我,無動於衷,彷彿我剛剛是對著牆壁說話。我在大學期間雙主修新聞與藝術,對藝術家的言行舉止或裝腔作勢,我了然於心。對我而言,我會善用左腦優勢來補右腦之不足。但我必須坦承,越是傾向右腦主導的藝術家,他們的管理與掌控力則越差,這情況幾乎屢見不爽,鮮少有例外。

數十年來,我深入解構無數「右腦思維過剩,左腦思維不足」的藝術家。一九八零年代初期,透過我合作共事的南加州大學,我曾帶了兩位中國藝術家到美國,最終,他們在美國大放異彩且成功移民、定居下來。

我之前那間位於雲南藏區中甸山上的房子,這段時間騰出空間,讓茲易與一位女藝術家傅宇住下。三層樓的木頭別墅,居高臨下,俯瞰一座松木林與魚池,整個傾斜而下的場景與系列建築、展館與涼亭,兼具各種使用功能,包括作家或作曲家的住宿地、多功能大廳與展覽博物館。所有共十一座建築體,組合而成中國探險學會的中甸中心,就位於大家所熟知的香格里拉外圍。我已搬到山下的一間單人房小屋,空間足夠有餘,還可讓我無需再為三餐或接見訪客,而每天上山下山好幾回。

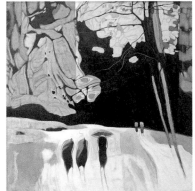
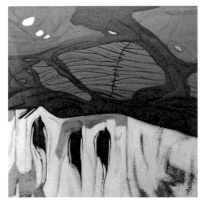

Kyaw Zay Yar's surrealistic paintings / 郭扎雅的超現實畫作

和茲易說話時，我有些猶豫，最終還是隱約其辭，把心中不滿的具體緣由，壓下不說。我不是個愛喝酒的人，但在別墅廚房內，我收藏了一些好酒：威士忌、白蘭地、葡萄酒、中國私釀酒等，隨時備好與來訪友人小酌。我把這些酒收在廚房角落已長達二十年。當我一查，發現酒瓶內都空了。茲易是出了名的千杯不醉，也可以說好酒貪杯。但茲易也是個令人非常欣賞、很想舉薦的鬼才藝術家，我們正為他籌辦中國探險學會前所未有的客席藝術家計劃。

我在緬甸撣邦高原的茵萊湖把茲易的其中一幅作品買走之後，緬甸中心的經理珊卓拉首先在仰光聯絡到他。茲易徵詢，能否也讓同為藝術家的妹妹一起跟過來，我同意了，把她也帶來。但後來才發現，其實傅宇不是他妹妹，而是茲易的女友，同時也是位技藝精湛的畫家，而且總是迎合取悅茲易。茲易自父母雙亡，便跑至仰光一所藝術學院學習。他來自緬甸西部若開邦 (Rakhine)——近期在國際間因驅趕羅興亞人事件，或如人所言，要他們自主出走而臭名遠播的若開邦——至今仍陷入軍人與當地民兵組織之間的混戰。

Artist residency house /
為客席藝術家提供的房子
Zhongdian Center kiosks / 中甸中心涼亭

茲易的家庭非常貧困，無力支持他完成藝術學院的學習。他窮得只能吃同學每天兩餐剩下的殘羹冷飯，週末同學們回家了，他便只能忍飢受餓，這狀況大家都知道。或許是如此食不果腹的極度匱乏，使他發展出扭曲的習慣：偷竊成性，同時是個熟練的拾荒者。他菸不離手的習慣，不僅為他的健康帶來警號，同時也大幅縮減他原來旺盛的創作力。

茲易擅於使用郵票或回收的舊紙鈔來創作。他早期畫作的靈感，深受自身家園所歷經的不公義與社會問題所啟發，於是，他的作品主題，離不開改革與激進的色彩。但要找到欣賞這類藝術畫作的買主，其實並不容易。還好，中國探險學會首度嘗試為他安排客席藝術家的計劃，還算順利，雖然他們的用餐與睡眠時間實在完全「異於常人」。

接下來，我們安排在緬甸的探險船上和位於茵萊湖的中心接待兩位藝術家。很慶幸的是，一起同行的傅宇，其實也是個才華橫溢的藝術家，她作品中的孩子，令人賞心悅目，而她的水漬油畫也漸入佳境，越來越令人驚艷。另一個預料之外的驚喜是傅宇的家人。原來她父親和他三個女兒，全是藝術家。我記得第一次與傅宇見面時，是在她蒙育瓦 (Monywa) 後巷一間簡陋不堪的屋子裡，距離第二大城曼德勒 (Mandalay) 西邊，約需兩小時車程。她狹小的房間裡，畫架放在床旁，床上是她捲縮身子作畫的地方，

眼前一幕與我的想象，其實相去不遠。後來認識了她在曼德勒大學教授雕塑的姐姐瑞真喇 *(Swe Zin Latt)*，我其實一點兒也不驚訝她們三姐妹的藝術天賦；我以為，在藝術家父親耳濡目染下，孩子們自然浸淫在藝術天地中成長；但實則不然，原來父親的藝術之路走得曲折。

傅宇的父親尤蘇廷雖早有藝術家夢想，但認清事實的他，知道堅持藝術夢想恐怕難以將三個女兒拉拔長大；於是，尤蘇廷保有一份穩定工作，維持家計，直到三個女兒長大並陸續成了藝術工作者之後，這位父親才終於放心轉換跑道，成為家中最後一個全心投入藝術工作的家庭成員；並擅長以天然玉石來雕塑。

但是，並非所有藝術家都像傅宇一家人那般，全心為藝術奉獻。我之前收藏了三幅郭扎雅 *(Kyaw Zay Yar)* 的畫作，我欣賞他超寫實風格的風景畫，尤其他對佛教僧侶人物的誇大詮釋法，獨樹一幟；而值得一提的是，郭扎雅自己也曾當過出家和尚。他偶爾也使用金葉片來當他作品的元素，使人聯想起早期佛教的壁畫藝術。我有意邀請他成為我們的客席藝術家，才正想著要聯繫他，便獲知他被家

Phyu with paintings /
傅宇與她的畫作

人關在家裡，已有四年不作畫了。他沉陷嚴重毒癮中，失魂喪魄般恍惚的身心，或許造就了他色彩炫目而迷離的藝術創作。我決定把他最後剩下的三幅畫作都買下。

中國探險學會的實驗性新模式，靈感來自探險精神，在學會有發展項目和運作的國家，為藝術家提供相應的支援。經過精挑細選的少數新晉藝術家將獲邀請成為客席藝術家，在中國探險學會於中國、緬甸、菲律賓和香港的場所駐留創作。

這些藝術家可以各種多元媒介進行創作，向各界展示他們的作品，甚至進一步把作品出售至中國探險學會的上層支持者。中國探險學會以經紀機構的角色，將一般的中介費用轉匯至藝術家的故鄉，以此支持非營利的保育計劃。中國探險學會的朋友買到的這些畫作，也將有機會借出在未來的展覽中展出。

中國探險學會擁有幾個基地，都在寧謐幽靜處；既然萬事俱備，我們開始想，不如善用空間，讓這些地方發揮最大用處，讓作家與音樂及藝術創作者可以住在優美環境中，或許能激發他們泉湧

Portrait using currency of General Aung San / 以鈔票拼貼出翁山蘇姬
Swe Zin Latt's sculptures / 瑞真喇的雕塑

的靈思。於是，二零一九年，我們啟動了試驗計劃，一次邀請兩位客席藝術家，就從緬甸的這兩位開始。

在此計劃下，我們希望從中國探險學會長期駐足的地方，包括不丹、菲律賓、寮國等鄰近國家，陸續邀請不同藝術家。而長遠看來，這項計劃將促使亞洲區發展中國家的藝術家之間，建立起橫向連結。我們的目標，是要發掘新晉、有才氣但韜光晦跡的藝術家，打開他們在故鄉以外的知名度，為他們搭建更大的舞台、接觸更多的受眾，無論對象是蒐藏家或展覽來賓。

我們並不期待要長期為這些藝術家代言，我們只要拋磚引玉，讓他們的作品與知名度更廣為人知。按照下一檔期的規劃，我已經開始審核不丹的藝術家。後續我也希望將藝術創作形態擴大至更原始樸質的風格，譬如薩滿教藝術家的創作，或由一群住在菲律賓南方巴拉望 (Palawan) 叢林內、少至三百人的巴塔克族來創作。

巴塔克人大多嗜酒如命，但他們喝的不會是我的酒。因為他們仰頭大喝的不是瓶子裡倒出來的甘露，而是取自大自然，從椰子樹摘下、發酵而成的瓊漿玉液。這個我們不缺，我們在巴拉望自己基地的椰子樹，至少也有上千棵吧！

Mao with Mao Rmb /
毛澤東與展示他頭像的人民幣
It doesn't matter whether a cat is white or black, as
long as it catches mice. /
不管黑貓白貓，能捉到老鼠就是好貓

中
國
探
險
學
會
的
新
家

A NEW CERS HOUSE

Mandalay, Myanmar – March 20, 2020

A NEW CERS HOUSE
Along a tributary of the Irrawaddy

Almost seven years ago, CERS launched the HM Explorer, a 106-foot river vessel with seven air-conditioned guest cabins. This purpose-built boat allowed CERS to explore waterways of Myanmar, in particular the upper Irrawaddy and its main tributary the Chindwin River. To date, many river trips have been conducted each year, including several cruises involving students and guests.

All along, since 2013 when the boat was first commissioned into service, I have wanted to find a permanent home to moor this very important CERS exploration boat. Numerous trips were taken just to locate an ideal piece of land as our home and center near Mandalay. Finally, an affordable lot was identified and purchased, and a three-story house built to accommodate several functions for the organization, beyond being only a boat base. A second house construction can also begin as of 2021.

The new CERS Mandalay House is located in Thapatetan Village on the Dokhtawaddy River,, less than thirty minutes by car from the airport and a mere five minutes cruise down to the main channel of the Irrawaddy River. This is where the two train and car bridges connect neighboring

Rear deck and bedroom / 後方的露天平台與睡房   2/F office with balcony / 二樓辦公室與陽台

Sagaing Division to Mandalay, second largest city of Myanmar. The village has around 80 families, predominantly involved in pottery making and weaving of longyi, the daily costume of traditional Burmese people.

From today, this new house begins to function as the main CERS office in Myanmar, with accommodations for our country manager, field scientist, local staff and visiting colleagues. Much of our expedition and scientific equipment have now been relocated from our boat to this new house. Front balconies on each floor offer an unobstructed view of the beautiful Mandalay sunset, and a back deck graces our morning wake up with a perfect sunrise.

Birds and squirrels are plentiful as the house is surrounded by tall mango trees. The songs of birds and the rhythm of the weaving machines create a most beautiful symphony to accompany us as we write or work over a map to plan our next expedition into the vast natural and cultural diversity of this wonderful ancient country.

(CERS would like to thank Ester Goelkel and her family Moritz Foundation for their support in making this CERS house a reality)

中國探險學會的新家 在伊洛瓦底江支流

幾乎是七年前的事了，中國探險學會啟動專用探險船「HM 探險家號」的首航禮，106 呎長的大船，內有七間冷氣雙人客房。這艘探險船的主要目的，是要讓中國探險學會在緬甸各水域河流中，自由探索，尤其是伊洛瓦底江上游，與其最大支流欽敦江 (Chindwin River)。直至今日，我們每一年都完成好幾趟河流探索之旅，除了學會的工作人員，其中幾次，我們還帶了學生與訪客一起參與。

打從二零一三年探險船啟動首航之初，我心中其實一直想著要為這艘重要的大船，找到安身立命的停靠之處，讓它不必在外「漂泊不定」。我們來回徘徊好幾趟，只為在緬甸第二大城曼德勒 (Mandalay) 附近，覓得理想之地，作為我們的家與學會中心。最終，我們找到並購入價格合理的土地，除了作為大船停泊的基地，更興建了一間三層樓房子，第二棟房子也在 2021 年可以開始動工了，可以同時滿足學會不同活動的需求。

中國探險學會在曼德勒的新家，就位於米界河 (Dokhtawaddy River) 上的塔巴特坦村 (Thapatetan)，距離機場不到三十分鐘車程，不需五分鐘就能「溜」到伊洛瓦底江的主要河道。這也是銜接鄰近的實皆省 (Sagaing Division) 到曼德勒的鐵軌與車橋交匯處。塔巴特坦村只有大約八十戶家庭，居民主要以陶器製作與編織緬甸傳統服飾「籠基」(longyi) 維生。

1/F meeting room / 一樓會議室
Map and display / 地圖與展示
HM Explorer and new house / 探險船「HM 探險家號」與新家

從今天起，中國探險學會的這間新房子，不僅是我們在緬甸的主要辦公室，同時也是我們區經理、田野科學家、當地員工與訪問同仁的住宿。原來放置在船上的探險裝備與科研設備，現在也都搬到新辦公室裡。每一層樓的前陽台，都可以瞥見曼德勒最目眩神迷的夕陽與黃昏；而後方的露天平台，則以最完美的旭日東升，來迎接我們的晨起時光。

樹大根深的芒果樹，環繞房子四周，雀鳥與松鼠是常客。蟲鳴鳥叫與織布機聲，交匯成悅耳的交響樂，我們徜徉其間，或書寫，或圍著地圖規劃下一趟途程，探索這美麗古國的自然與文化的多元勝境。

（中國探險學會要特別感謝 Ester Goelkel 與其家族 Moritz 基金會的支持，使中國探險學會的新居得以落成，夢想成真。）

冷
古
寺

LENGGU MONASTERY

Hong Kong – May 19, 2020

LENGGU MONASTERY
A tiny CERS project hidden inside a sacred mountain

From the satellite image on my iPad, our route is penetrating into the heart of the high snow range surrounding what is Ge Nyen sacred mountain (6204 meters). The circular cluster of snowfields somewhat resembles petals of a lotus. A trail with peaks on both sides was what we used as access into the mountain. Beside it was a clear and pristine river cascading down from glaciers and alpine lakes. Between 2017 and 2019, twice, my team and I entered this remote mountain fastness.

The occasional meadows are like patches of green carpet where the gushing river would momentarily become a quiet calm stream as it flows through the valley. Rhubarb rising high in prime yellow color, with some in red as it becomes ripe, dotted the valley floor. They grow most abundantly near the many streams feeding the river. These alpine plants, with short growing season yet rising tall at high elevation, are an important ingredient for both traditional Tibetan and Chinese medicine.

Indeed, during the middle ages, Rhubarb from China, predominantly from the Tibetan plateau, was considered by people from the Middle East and Europe to be such a potent drug for all ailments that huge amounts were exported. It was recorded in an account from the 14th century in the

Ming Dynasty that in one month alone, of the 600 camels arriving at Samarkand, 300 were carrying rhubarb – or the equivalent of 100 tons. Here, however, they are left to decay, withering as summer passes.

It is also in these meadows yaks roam, grazing among the flowers. Some of them have colored ribbons tied to their necks or horns, with a full coat of fur much thicker than the usual yak we see. These are the more sacred among yaks, freed by local Tibetans as offerings to the mountain gods.

It is among such idyllic natural landscapes that the ancient Lenggu monastery is located, at an elevation of 4151 meters, set among pine and fir forests. The jade peaks, some like knives piercing into heaven, sit majestically like armed guardians protecting this largely forgotten temple. Just a couple hours hike to the south is one of the very busy caravan routes historically providing access between the plain of Chengdu through to Litang, then Batang, and into Tibet.

A small village, Lamaya, used to witness caravans passing, at times numbering over a hundred pack animals. Villagers would hear the bell of the leading mule approaching, as the long train of horses and mules passed through the village. Lamaya not only offers respite and shelter for a night during a long journey, the villagers would also serve as caravan helpers

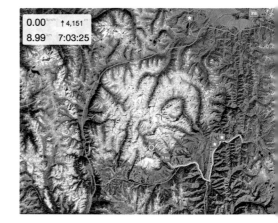

Ge Nyen and route from space /
格聶峰與路徑的衛星圖
Peaks around Ge Nyen / 格聶峰的群峰

in a relay toward the next stage stop. Others would make a little money supplying grain and fodder for the draft animals.

Today, though the trade caravans are long gone, Lamaya still provide a service for us latecomers. It is here that we organize horses to take us to Lenggu monastery and beyond. We would drive ahead with our fleet of Land Rovers and rendezvous at the foot of the sacred mountain the following morning. There, near the newer and much larger Lenggu monastery, ruled by a different Rinpoche than the one overseeing the old monastery, would be where we set our base camp, at an elevation of 3902 meters.

There are literally hundreds and thousands of big and small Tibetan monasteries and temples throughout the plateau. Few people, not even Tibetan Buddhists, would know what is special about this Lenggu monastery, with only one main assembly hall rebuilt in the 1980s and much of the monks' quarters surrounding it in dilapidated condition.

Freed yak / 自由的犛牛
Starting our march / 開始我們的徒步之旅
Riding toward Lenggu monastery / 騎馬往冷古寺出發

Lenggu monastery, meaning "Cold and Old" in Chinese, was first founded in 1164 by the First Karmapa, founder of the Karma Kagyu branch of Tibetan Buddhism. Today that lineage is into its 17th generation, with the current Karmapa blessing his adherents and the public both with political and religious intrigues. I had the great fortune of being invited as a special guest at his enthronement in Tsurphu monastery outside of Lhasa in September 1992 when he was seven years old. Later I met him again when he was living in Dharamshala under Indian "protection."

The Lenggu monastery was turned into a Gelug or Yellow Sect monastery by the year 1690, something quite common as what was then the newest sect of Tibetan Buddhism became the most dominating religious force throughout much of the Tibetan plateau under the Fifth Dalai Lama. At its peak, Lenggu had over 2000 resident monks, but today it has only a handful of monks, with the monastery literally befits its name, cold and old.

My latest visit came in June 2019, when I invited a small group of friends from Bhutan to join me. Among them were Ashi Kesang Choden Wangchuk, a princess from the Royal Family together with her two sons, a Bhutanese monk Sonam, and Ugyen, a long-time friend. Tashi Rinpoche, a direct descendent of the 7th Dalai Lama's family in Litang, came along to facilitate our visit. CERS was fortunate to provide support some years ago to repair and restore the house where the 7th Dalai was born. Thus the Rinpoche and CERS have become close friends.

The march, then a ride into the heart of Ge Nyen mountain was awe-inspiring. The scenic beauty of nature captivated our imagination as if on way to a heavenly enclave. The floating clouds silhouetting cliffs and peaks was mesmerizing. It took about two hours from base camp when the monastery revealed itself, sitting on a sloping hill. As we approached a white pagoda, we saw a herd of Blue Sheep grazing at the base of it. Without dismounting from our horses, we took pictures while these usually-shy animals seemed totally oblivious to our presence. Indeed,

such a balance of nature and human can only be found in the remotest corners of the earth now.

We had brought along our picnic lunch and entered a stone house to enjoy some buttered tea served by two local monks. I decided to eat my lunch outside and enjoy the scenery at a broken stone house with a walled-in garden. It has a wonderful view of both the sacred Ge Nyen mountain as well as a cliff on the other side.

As curiosity drove me, I went inside the house with broken door and windows. Part of the wall and roof had collapsed. Asking the two local monks, they said the house was formerly used for meditation but had long been abandoned. Restoring it would require quite some effort given how far away the monastery is from the road.

It seemed a nice small project just perfect for CERS to leave a little impact behind. I have often repeated a notion to our student interns, "So you have seen many places, have any of these places seen you?" To

Blue Sheep at Lengu / 冷古寺的西藏岩羊
Rhubarb blooming / 大黃盛放
Peaks & glaciers / 群峰與冰川

illustrate my point, I have grown to love small projects, since they can become an inspiration for the younger generation who may have less patience and fewer resources to start larger and more long-term undertakings. So, this meditation house would be another case study for us.

Furthermore, it helped demonstrate my other notion that big things attract the eyes, while small things touch the heart. Indeed, CERS has supported several small projects, two in Tibet alone, without anyone knowing about it. Without much fanfare, and through Tashi Rinpoche as our proxy, we committed CERS to paying for the repair of this small stone house on the edge of Lenggu monastery.

Today, less than a year later, the roof, walls and garden are done. The little bit of work remaining would be to replace the door and windows. I look forward to returning soon to spend a night in it, perhaps meditating under the shadow of sacred Ge Nyen, while the Blue Sheep graze quietly in our yard.

Dilapidated stone house / 殘破不堪的石頭屋

New Lenggu monastery / 新的冷古寺

冷古寺

中國探險學會深藏於神山裡的小計劃

從 *iPad* 上顯示的衛星影象定位判斷，我們的路線，不偏不倚穿越格聶峰周邊的中心點，這座海拔高度 *6204* 公尺的神山，高聳入雲；四圍白皚皚一片雪原，層層堆疊的積雪封霜，仿若蓮花瓣葉。兩座山巔之間的路徑，是我們進入神山的入口。一旁是滔滔汩汩的河流，從高山湖與冰川傾瀉而下。掐指一算，我和團隊在二零一七年與二零一九年曾先後兩次來過這個偏遠山區。

偶然瞥見的綠地，就像小片小片的綠色地毯上；一旁湍急奔流的河水，有時也化身為澄澈平靜的溪水，不起波瀾地流經河谷。多年生草本植物大黃，貌如其名，原黃色，葉大柄粗，成熟時轉紅，點綴野外谷地；尤其近溪流處的大黃，長得特別枝繁葉茂。這些高山植物在極短的生長季節裡，奮力在高海拔山區長好長高，是傳統西藏與中藥的重要藥材。

中世紀時，中國的大黃其實源自西藏高原，被中東與歐洲視為可治百病的優質藥材而需求大增，出口量也水漲船高。十四世紀時，當時的明代朝廷曾有一筆賬目記錄，單一個月內，抵達撒馬爾罕 (Samarkand) 的六百隻駱駝，其中為數一半的三百隻都馱運大黃，相當於一百噸之多。不過，今不如昔，眼前的大黃只能在夏去秋來時，枯萎衰殘。

Ge Nyen and its glacier / 格聶峰與冰川　　　　High camp a day above Lenggu / 冷古寺高原露營

犛牛也在同一片草地與花叢間，遊走吃草。有些犛牛的脖子或角上被繫上彩帶，披上比一般犛牛還要厚實的皮毛。這些犛牛中的犛牛，被當地藏民賦予「自由身」而免受屠殺，牠們是獻予山神的「神犛」，身份尊貴。

古老的冷古寺，位於海拔高度 4151 公尺，被松木與冷杉林環抱，藏於得天獨厚的田園景致之中。蒼翠如玉石的山巔，遠看像插入天堂的刀刃，莊嚴而凜凜然地端坐高處，仿若全副武裝的守衛，悉心守護這座被遺忘人間的大廟宇。往南爬升數小時不久，便是一條曾經車水馬龍的繁忙古道——從成都平地，取道理塘縣，再穿越巴塘縣，進入西藏的必經之路。

當地一座小村落喇嘛埡鄉，一直以來見證了這條歷史古道的興衰，最輝煌時曾有每隊上百頭的馬幫隊馱運進出，川流不息。隨著領頭騾趨近時，鄉民會聽到陣陣鈴聲，那是長長的騾馬運輸隊經過村莊的時候。跋山涉水後，人困馬乏，喇嘛埡鄉除了提供運輸隊投宿與休憩之處，鄉民也扮演起運輸隊的幫手，協助調度與下一段旅途相關的行程。此外，鄉民也可藉此機會為牲畜預備穀物飼料，賺些小錢。

Camp in view of new monastery /
帳篷外可看見新寺院
Restored house with Tashi Rinpoche /
扎西仁波切與修復後的房子

雖然今天所謂的荒漠馬幫古道早已在歷史時空中，消失殆盡；但今天，喇嘛埡鄉仍為我們這群遲到的訪客提供服務。我們就在當地安排了馬隊，準備將我們載至冷古寺與更遠的地方。隔天一早，再以我們的越野路虎車隊驅車跟上，至神山山腳下會合。我們就在靠近冷古寺旁一處 3902 公尺的高地上，扎營安頓。這是一座更新、更大的冷古寺，駐寺的仁波切，已經不是之前在舊寺掌舵的那位主持。

西藏高原上的大小寺廟成千上萬，絕非誇大其詞。大部分人對冷古寺的獨特之處不知所以，即便藏族佛教徒也不甚了了；人們大概只知道，其中一座經堂在一九八零年重建，當時還有許多僧侶院舍圍繞在殘破不堪的廟宇四周。

冷古寺的中文原意帶有「冷與古」之含義，一一六四年由藏傳佛教的支派噶瑪噶舉派第一世噶瑪巴所創建。如今，這段宗派轉世脈絡，已傳承至第十七代，現今的噶瑪巴活躍於各種政治與宗教場合上，經常公開對追隨群眾加持與祝福。我很榮幸曾在一九九二年九月時，以貴賓身份受邀至拉薩外的楚布寺，參加大寶法王噶瑪巴的坐床儀式，當年噶瑪巴只有七歲。多年以後再見他時，他已轉移居住地至達蘭薩拉 (Dharamsala)，接受印度「庇護」。

Cliff massif / 山崖峭壁

一六九零年，冷古寺轉為格魯派（僧侶頭戴黃帽因此也被稱為黃教）主持，這在當年的時代背景下，是極為普遍的狀況。格魯派作為當年藏傳佛教的新興宗派，在第五世達賴喇嘛的領導下，確立了它在西藏高原上最為主導的宗教地位。冷古寺最鼎盛時，有超過兩千位住寺僧侶，對比今天寺院內的寥寥幾位僧人，冷古寺成了名符其實、「又冷又古」的寺廟。

我最近期的訪視，是二零一九年六月，當時我邀請了不丹的一群朋友一起過來。這一行人包括不丹皇室阿禧格桑雀登 (Ashi Kesang Choden Wangchuk) 公主，與公主的兩位兒子，還有一名不丹僧侶蘇南，以及多年老友尤研。理塘縣的第七世達賴喇嘛直系扎西仁波切也特別過來參與我們的旅程。與扎西仁波切的因緣得從數年前說起，當時中國探險學會有幸支援修復與保護七世達賴出生的房子，自此我們便成了親近的好友。

這段前進格聶峰中心的徒步及騎馬旅程，觸目所及，都是震懾人心的壯闊宏偉之景。大自然刻鑿的絕美氣勢，與一路的風月無邊，驅使我們的想象力馳騁，腳下的每一步，仿若走向天堂般的飛地秘境。浮雲映襯下的峭壁與山峰，看得人心醉神迷。從我們駐扎的營區到瞥見屹立緩坡上的冷古寺，約需兩小時。抵達一座白色佛塔時，眼前一群高山岩羊正在吃草。我們繼續騎乘馬上，抓緊機會拍照，這些本性害羞的岩羊竟對我們的存在毫無所覺，不躲不逃。我心想，自然界與人類之間和諧共處的平衡之美，如今恐怕只存在於地球上最山窮水盡的遙遠角落裡。

我們隨身帶了野餐食物，走進一間石頭房子，享受兩位僧侶為我們準備的酥油茶。我心血來潮，決定走到一間殘毀不全的石頭屋，在屋外一座別有洞天的圍牆花園，邊欣

賞滿園美景邊用餐。這裡是觀賞格聶峰的絕佳角度，連另一邊的懸崖峭壁也一覽無遺。

我的好奇心驅使我推開破舊的門與窗，走進屋內。有些牆壁與屋瓦已倒塌。我詢問兩位當地僧侶，他們說那房子原是冥想閉關的禪修所在，但已被棄置好一段時間了。由於寺院在遙遠的另一頭，因此，若要修復重建，想必得耗時費力。

但這對中國探險學會而言，恰好是力所能及的計劃，而且能為當地留下一份饒富意義的微薄貢獻。我經常對實習學生反覆提問一個觀念：「你們已經見識了許多地方，但這些地方是否認識你？」請容我解釋這想法：我向來喜歡小計劃，因為務實可行的小計劃往往可以啟發年輕一代——他們耐心不足又缺乏啟動長遠大抱負的資源。所以，這間靜思小屋，或可成為我們的研究個案。

除此以外，這個行動也落實我的另一個理念：大東西引人矚目，但小東西觸動心靈。中國探險學會確實支持不少「小而美」的計劃與行動，單在西藏已經有兩項，鮮為人知。接下來，中國探險學會負責支付這間小石屋的維修費，我們不打算大張旗鼓地高調宣揚，只委託扎西仁波切全權代為處理，重整這座位於冷古寺邊陲的小屋。

距今還不滿一年，小石屋的屋瓦、牆壁與花園都已修復完工。只剩小部分更換門窗的工作，便大功告成。多麼希望可以很快再回來，可以在這裡留宿一晚，或許在格聶峰的山影下冥想，會不會那時，西藏岩羊也在院子裡安靜凝視我？

高
原
上
的
賽
馬

HORSE RACING ON THE HIGH PLATEAU

Hong Kong – May 21, 2020

HORSE RACING ON THE HIGH PLATEAU
A photo essay

Today, it is next to impossible to have any ethnic festival or ceremony in China without drawing a crowd of tourists, reporters, and photographers from outside, be they local or foreign. Any larger such event would come with a contingent of government officials, police escort, security detail, and spectators.

But that kind of untainted festival was precisely what the CERS team ran into a year ago - an unknown horse-racing event almost coinciding in time with Litang County's famous once-a-year horse racing festival. This smaller cousin happened just some 80 kilometers beyond Litang at the village of Lamaya, hidden inside the valley of Ranrika, a settlement of may be less than a couple hundred families, yet with a rather imposing monastery.

We ran into this event totally by chance, on our way to the sacred mountain of Ge Nyen. After leaving Lamaya and heading into the hills on a windy and circuitous dirt road, we scaled a mountain to reach our base camp at the foot of Ge Nyen. While descending the mountain we saw Tibetans setting up a big tent in the pasture and stopped to inquire. They invited us to come back

Horse honored / 馬匹頒獲殊榮

in the morning to join their yearly event, organized locally to celebrate the arrival of summer. So the next morning we left camp early and drove back to the valley.

The photo portfolio thus recorded is the most simple and accurate documentation of a raw Tibetan horse-racing festival I have ever seen over a period of forty years on the plateau. Competitors were divided into teams, racing from start to finish for a distance of about 250 meters. Most riders rode bareback though a few had colorful saddle blanket and fewer yet used a wooden Tibetan saddle. They are mainly young riders, teenagers or those in their 20s and at most 30s. A few were even monks, though riding with their long robes off. Spectators, all locals except for our team, were as spectacular and colorful as the riders were.

As each group of riders dashed across the finish line, a high monk was on hand to put a golden khata, a long ceremonial scarf, over the neck of the winning horses. Prize money in the hundreds of RMB were handed out to the winners. Other highlights of the races involved acrobatics on horseback, with the riders dipping deeply sideways or even backwards on a galloping horse to pick up pieces of khata laid on the ground. Some of the best riders could even pick up smaller objects in the form of special prizes laid on the pasture.

Archery on horseback came as the finale of the afternoon, and the crowd cheered horses stampeding across the field while their riders took aim and shot arrows at a target placed on the ground.

The entire event lasted from around 10am to 3pm when people started dispersing and the meadow returned to peace as if nothing had happened. And peace would remain until perhaps a year later, when they would gather again on this day in June.

Monk spectators / 僧人觀眾
Family spectators / 一家人的觀眾
Galloping horses / 馬匹競賽

Ride & shoot / 策馬與開弓
Neck to neck race / 叮噹馬頭的賽事

高原上的賽馬
專題攝影

今天，舉凡中國境內籌辦任何民族傳統節慶，無不吸引國內外絡繹不絕的遊客、記者與攝影師前來。類似重量級活動也不乏政府官員出席，與隨之出動的大批警力維護和安檢，加上川流不息的群眾，場面總是熙攘熱鬧。

一年前，中國探險學會竟與一場不為人知的賽馬活動，不期而遇。活動時間恰好與理塘縣一年一度的賽馬節慶幾乎同步舉辦。這場規模較小的賽馬活動地點，距離理塘縣八十公里以外的喇嘛埡村——一個藏身然日卡山谷的村落——人口不多，只有零星約兩百戶家庭，但村裡有座氣勢雄偉的大寺院。

這完全是一場不在行程中的意外驚喜。那一天，我們離開喇嘛埡村，動身前往格聶神山。一路風沙蔽天、蜿蜒曲折，我們的目標是爬上山後的扎營所在。下坡路段途中，我們看見藏民在一片牧場搭起大帳篷，於是駐足，好奇探問。他們邀請我們隔天早晨過來，參加他們為了迎接夏天而自行舉辦的年度活動。因此，我們隔日早早便離開營地，驅車折返山谷。

這是我過去四十幾年來，在西藏高原拍攝過最樸實無華、最原始自然的藏民賽馬影象記錄。選手們被分成不同隊伍，從起點至終點，快馬加鞭奔馳約兩百五十公尺。大部分選手採無鞍騎乘，但還是有少部分騎士使用色彩斑斕的馬鞍座氈，我還看到有選手

甚至把木製的西藏馬鞍都派上用場了。現場馬背上縱馬疾馳的，主要是年輕騎士、青少年或年齡層介於二十到三十之間的青壯年；還有少數僧侶也展現騎馬英姿，任由長袍隨風飛揚。觀禮群眾中，除了我們這群外來客之外，都是當地居民；草皮上的觀眾與馬背上的騎手一樣引人矚目，五彩繽紛之亮麗，不相上下。

當每一隊伍往終點線衝刺時，勝出的那位，有高僧親手獻上黃金哈達 (khata) 披巾，掛在獲勝的馬頸上，那是藏族表達崇高敬意的傳統禮節；另外還贈上數百人民幣獎金予獲勝騎士。此外，其他令人耳目一新的競賽還包括，馬背上耍雜技——騎士在飛奔中的馬背上，身體深深地傾側，又或仰身往後，把地上的哈達撿起來。有些訓練有素的騎士，甚至可以輕鬆撿起那些以「特別獎」的形式放在牧場上的小東西，誰有能力撿起，禮物就歸誰。

馬背上射箭，是下午活動落幕前的重頭戲。當騎士一邊策馬猛衝一邊瞄準草地上設好的標物準備射擊時，圍觀群眾難掩激動之情，而興奮歡呼。

整場活動從上午十點延續至下午三點結束。曲終人散後，草原復歸平靜，彷彿剛剛所有歡聲雷動，都不曾發生過。我想，或許如此平靜祥和，將持續至一年後吧，直等明年此時的六月夏至，大家再回到草地上歡聚。

Profile of Tibetan / 藏人的側面人像
Catching up / 迎頭趕上
Michael Jackson of Tibet / 西藏的麥可‧傑克森

戰爭的藝術

THE ART OF WAR

75th Anniversary of Japan's surrender in WWII - Hong Kong

THE ART OF WAR
A Japanese artist in war time China

The Art of War of my title is not about the seminal work of Sun Tzu (500BC), the Chinese military strategist, but more literally about artists who painted during the War.

Hoan Kosugi (小杉放庵 , 1881 - 1964) was a renowned Japanese painter who spanned the 19th and 20th century. Today, there is a nice museum named after him and displaying his works of art in Nikko Japan, the place of his birth.

Kosugi was a war artist as early as the Russo-Japanese War between 1904-05 as that engagement took place in Manchuria of China. At the time Kosugi was barely 23 years old and was attached to the military as an artist. Based on his training, he was painting in a western style, using oil and watercolor as his media.

Not all military artists would excel and become so famous. My copy of the fourth volume of a Japanese book of illustrations of the Russo-Japanese War published in 1905 features 65 illustrations by over two dozen artists, and Kosugi's work is not even included among them once.

Russians coming for surrender near Mukden /
俄軍在天奉附近求降

As expected, the paintings depict the horror of the battlefield and the bravery and heroism of the Japanese soldiers. The collection even displays the benevolence of the Japanese in dealing with the defeated. The Russians are portrayed in a very different light.

During the war between Japan and China, Kosugi was again invited to visit China in 1940. This time, however, his trip was not military related; he came as a guest of the Central China Railway Company operated by the Japanese. Kosugi was then into his late fifties. His style had changed to that of Chinese ink painting, forgoing his earlier western training.

Going through his very rare album with 46 paintings that only 350 copies were made (I have copy Number 5), I immediately took a liking with his sketches though many were done without color. As a student, I double-majored in Journalism and Art. I could quickly see the similarities of Kosugi's work to several later Chinese artists. Though

Defeated Russians eating horse flesh in their
retreat / 戰敗俄軍在撤退路上吃馬肉充饑
Japanese soldiers rescuing some Russians in
the Harbour of Port Arthur /
日本士兵在亞瑟港救起俄軍

whether they were affected by Kosugi I cannot determine. Feng Zikai (1898-1975) portrayal of simple village life and people perhaps has the greatest similarities. Followed somewhat closely are also style of Wu Guanzhong (1919-2010) in his rendition of landscape and trees. Even Song Wenzhi's (1919-1999) work bear some semblance.

The Japanese took hold of China's coastal area including Shanghai towards the end of 1937. Kosugi departed from Tokyo on April 5, 1940 and arrived in Shanghai shortly after. His early notes and diary described a bombed out city. From a hill, he witnessed the massive destruction and noted that "not a single house was intact". As spring had arrived, new green plants were sprouting up among the rubble. People were searching among the ruins to find anything of the slightest value.

Since his account was written over a decade later in 1962, he reflected that Tokyo and other Japanese cities were soon to receive destruction hundreds of times worse than what he witnessed in China. He further noted that, in any war, there is no real winner, and mourned the sorrow and sadness after the war.

The first painting in his album South of the Yangtze depicts a street scene in Shanghai painted probably upon his arrival at the city, as it was signed

"Buddha's birthday," which should be April 8. A man facing the wall is shown bending slightly while urinating against a concrete military bunker. Though it may seem odd today, such a scene was once common, even when I visited Japan in the 1970s, if one were to walk into a side alley.

A second painting from April 9 shows ruins of a totally bombed-out Commercial Press building with a person shoveling through the rubble. In Kosugi's text, he mentions how he had always chosen books by Commercial Press when he needed to read any books published in Chinese, and sighed at the many books that must have been destroyed.

From a burnt city and a fortress, he mourns the scorched earth stained with the blood of both armies. Kosugi had visited China on several other occasions. The race course, now with a huge bomb crater, only brings back old memories of brighter days. There are Chinese "soldiers" and volunteers allowed to dig mass graves to bury those who died in battle. Other soldiers are involved in a game of "hand wrestling" with a six-foot-long pole in between.

The Chinese team members are readily defeated by the stronger Japanese soldiers. But the acrobatic jump of a thin guy wins a lot of applause and Kosugi surmised he might have studied the Shaolin monastic martial arts.

His next stop is Yangzhou, a most beautiful town east of Nanjing. He mentions the lonely spring day among willows and temples along the way, inspiring him to write down his own poem to describe the scene.

Low, low, low, willow of a lonely spring;
When will the temple bell chime once again.

He recalls the ancient story of "bound to the waist a hundred thousand cash, riding a crane to arrive in Yangzhou" used to describe the town as the ultimate destination even for the rich. But Kosugi follows by describing the decay and demise of the town after the spoil of war, and that only the beauty of the ladies remains. At the Five Pavilion Bridge with its kiosks by the Slender West Lake, he is relieved that reports of its destruction are not true, and praises the architectural beauty of the structure.

In Nanjing, he visits the temples and lakes of the capital city. A couple of rhymed poems ornament his description of Nanjing, and he quotes the late Tang poet Du Mu. He recounts a historic tale from the end of the Six

南京市のどこらか　四月御延日号

Dynasties when it fell to the Sui Dynasty a thousand years ago. The king was hiding from the enemy inside a well. When the danger was over, the king was pulled up with much difficulty as he seemed very weighty. It turned out that two of his female consorts were also hiding below and were hanging on to the king. Thus the well since was known as the "Rouge Well".

Next Kosugi follows the Grand Canal and reaches the town of Suzhou, where he visits and paints several famous sites; Huqui Pagoda, Sword Pond, and the most exquisite of Suzhou's gardens. Perhaps due to the serenity of Suzhou, it brings to mind for Kosugi a few more Chinese poems and prose - about a boatman and girl rower in love, or two lovers buried next to each other with two tree branches above reaching out to touch one another. His knowledge of ancient Chinese history and poetry is fully demonstrated here, perhaps an example of the Japanese literati of the age.

Between Jiaqing and Hangzhou, Kosugi notices the huge number of soldiers on alert after some recent engagement in the area. He mentions here that he was in Hangzhou before but over a decade has passed already. Though there is beauty still in the city, the atmosphere is very different now, being near a battlefront, too tense for him to feel fully relaxed and enjoy.

As an artist, Kosugi is delighted to be entertained for dinner by staff of the Xilan Seal Society, a renowned artist club. The famous Da Ya (Big Grace) Gallery and frame shop are another favorite place of his visit and he thanks his good fortune of being able to paint from this special location.

West Lake full moon of spring;

Da Ya filled my chest and breast.

As he is painting some final sketches, thundering sound of canon fire come from a distance. Birds fly off from tree tops and a few monks look up as the shells whistle overhead. Making art during this war reminds him of his younger days as an artist during the Russo-Japanese War. A beautiful spring sky is suddenly turned into dark stormy earth.

His traveling companion quietly laments, "Can't we all live in peace and shake hands with each other!" That's a thought Kosugi shares.

"In the midst of chaos there is also opportunity." Sun Tzu may not have had artists in mind when he wrote that, nonetheless he might have approved of serene portrayal of selected beauty even during war time. It seems apparent that Kosugi tried his best in this effort.

(These records are from the limited edition of an album with only 350 copies printed in 1962. In it are Kosugi's paintings done during the War in China. Copy Number 5 is now within the CERS collection of books)

戰爭的藝術

戰亂期旅中之日本藝術家

我的標題《戰爭的藝術》(The Art of War) 與公元前五百年完成的《孫子兵法》(英譯出版書名即 The Art of War)，絲毫無關，我要著墨的不是中國的對戰策略，而是以符合字面的意義，講述戰亂期間的藝術家故事。

小杉放庵 (1881~1964)，從十九世紀活到二十世紀的著名日本畫家。今天，日本在他的出生地——關東的日光市，成立了一間以小杉放庵為名的日光美術館，常年展出他的藝術作品。小杉放庵早在一九零四至零五年間的日俄戰爭中，便已是戰爭藝術家，當時那場戰役在中國滿洲爆發，年方二十三的小杉放庵，以藝術家身份隨軍出征。依照他的訓練與素養，他擅長西方風格的繪畫，油彩與水彩是他主要的創作媒材。

其實，並非每一位軍事藝術家都能像他那樣成就斐然、名聞遐邇。我手上有一本一九零五年出版的第四集日本畫冊，以詮釋日俄戰爭為主題，其中超過二十四位畫家的六十五幅作品中，找不到任何一張小杉放庵的畫作。一如所料，畫冊的作品大多描繪可驚可怖的戰場，也不免對日軍的勇猛與英雄主義形象，歌功頌德一番；其中甚至還以畫展示，日本如何以寬容大度來善待被擊敗的對手，並以明顯不同的角度與光線，來描繪俄羅斯人。

中日戰爭開打時，小杉放庵再度於一九四零年受邀前往中國，但這一次的訪問與軍事戰役無關，而是以貴賓身份，接受當時日本營運的「華中鐵道株式會社」之邀。小杉放庵當時已五十幾歲，繪畫風格有別於他早期的西洋美術訓練，而轉向中國水墨畫。

翻閱小杉放庵非常少見的作品集，裡頭僅有的四十六幅畫，只印製了三百五十冊（我手上一冊為第五號版本），我一見傾心，被他大部分幾乎沒有顏色的素描深深吸引。我大學時曾雙主修新聞與藝術，他的作品使我立刻想起幾位與他畫風接近的後期中國藝術家。至於這些後起之秀是否深受小杉放庵的影響，我無從判斷。豐子愷 (1898~1975) 對農村生活與平凡百姓的描繪，樸實簡約，與小杉放庵的寫實風格極其相似。吳冠中 (1919~2010) 獨樹一格的風景與樹木繪法，也十分接近小杉放庵的演繹手法。我甚至覺得宋文治 (1919~1999) 清幽淡雅的畫作，也與小杉放庵有幾分神似。

一直到一九三七年底之前，中國沿海區域包括上海，都被日本佔據。小杉放庵一九四零年四月五日從東京出發，旋即抵達上海。他早期的筆記與日記對戰亂下被炸毀的城市，多所著墨。從丘陵高處往下俯瞰，他瞥見戰後滿目瘡痍的斷壁殘垣，並寫下：「沒有一間房屋是完好無損的」。「春天來了，綠色嫩芽從碎石瓦礫堆中冒出頭。倖存者在廢墟中倉惶尋找沒有多大價值的東西。」

Admiral Togo seeing the surrendered Rear-Admiral Nebogatoff on board the Mikasa /
敵艦降伏

由於他的記錄大約在一九六二年才完成出版，因此他得以見識中國與日本的戰後情境，小杉放庵後來寫道，東京與其他日本城市隨即所遭受的摧毀與破壞，比他在中國所目睹的還要慘烈數百倍。他在記錄中提及，任何戰爭都不會有真正的贏家，並對戰後的苦情與悲傷表達深切的哀悼。

小杉放庵的畫集《江南畫冊》(South of the Yangtze)，第一張作品所描繪的，便是上海的一條街景，標註上「佛陀誕生」，推算起來應該是四月八日，若然，則這幅畫極有可能是他抵達上海不久便完成。畫中有個男人稍稍屈膝弓背，面對堅不可摧的軍事地堡撒尿。或許如此舉止現在看來很突兀，但那曾經是見怪不怪的尋常「街景」；我記得七十年代到日本時，若見有人鑽進一旁小巷，不必多想，準是隨地小便居多。

第二幅畫則繪於四月九日，畫面是被徹底炸毀的商務印書館大樓，有人在一片瓦礫中鏟著挖掘。小杉放庵的文字敘述中，提及他每每需要閱讀任何中文書籍時，都會挑選「商務印書館」出版的中文書，眼看多少書籍就此毀於一旦，他為此而哀歎惋惜。

從一座被燒毀的城市與堡壘，再到戰爭中沾染雙方血液的焦土政策──軍隊撤離前不惜摧毀殆盡的手段──都令他感傷沉痛。此外，小杉放庵也曾訪問中國的其他地方與場合；譬如曾經風光一時的賽馬場，而今已成大彈坑，他慨歎往日輝煌只能回味。當時許多中國「士兵」與志願者獲准挖掘大墳，將死於戰亂的亡者集體掩埋；而其他士兵則分成中日兩隊人馬，在六尺長桿之間赤手空拳進行「手部扭打」遊戲。中國隊隨時被孔武有力的日本士兵撂倒擊敗；但一名精瘦男士的特技彈跳卻贏得滿堂喝彩與掌聲，小杉放庵推測這名老兄可能在少林寺練過武功。

下一站，小杉放庵停留揚州，南京之東最美的城市。孤寂的春天，他漫步搖曳生姿的柳樹下，行經路旁寺廟時，頃刻間，善感的畫家靈思泉湧，於是提筆寫下詩詞，描繪當下情景。

寂寥春日，楊柳依依
古剎老鐘，何時再響

小杉放庵憶起老故事中形容揚州的一段字句：「腰纏十萬貫、騎鶴下揚州」；把揚州描繪成繁華迷人之地，腰纏錢財的富豪也迫不及待到揚州享樂去。話鋒一轉，小杉放庵隨即描繪起連天烽火後的城市，被摧毀得殘缺破敗，唯獨揚州美女，風華猶在。小杉放庵一聽揚州地標建築——瘦西湖上的五亭橋，其實稍早聽聞的毀損報告並不正確，頓時鬆了一口氣，他對這建築結構之典雅大器，讚不絕口。

來到南京時，小杉放庵參觀這座首府之城的廟宇與湖泊。小杉放庵對南京城幾段自成韻律的書寫與

描繪，還引經據典，引用了晚唐詩人杜牧的詩句。他還特別詳述一千年前從魏晉南北朝的亂世，過度到隋朝的朝廷事跡。當年陳後主為躲攻城敵軍而心生一計，跳進一口井避難。危機過後，眾人費勁千辛萬苦才把他從井裡拖上來，看來他體重不輕；但後來才驚覺躲進井裡的除了皇上陳後主，還包括兩位他最寵愛的嬪妃，嬪妃的胭脂沾染了井口，雖然歷史情節與實況多有出入，但自此這口井便成了家喻戶曉的「胭脂井」，流傳至今。

小杉放庵接續旅程，經大運河而抵達蘇州，他在這裡停留並在蘇州幾處有名景點完成幾幅作品；包括虎丘塔、劍池與雅緻精美的蘇州園林。或許蘇州景致水天一色，難以抗拒，小杉放庵又想起好幾位中國詩詞與散文的情愛故事——擺渡人與女子墜入愛河，或深愛的伴侶死後比鄰而葬，墳上還以兩三根樹枝伸向彼此，以表相互探觸與連結之意。小杉放庵對遠古中國歷史與詩詞信手拈來，鑽研了解之深，堪稱當代日本真正文人學士之典範。

在嘉興市與杭州市之間，自該區近日完成交戰協定以來，小杉放庵注意到當地開始有大批進入戒備狀態的軍人，整裝待發。他在此特別提及，自己十年前曾到過杭州。雖然城市的旖旎風光不減當年，但現在與戰場前線如此靠近，整個城市的氛圍已大不如前；對他而言，那股蠢蠢欲動的肅殺之氣讓他心神緊繃，難以放鬆心情，恣意享受。

身為藝術家，能受著名藝術社團「西泠印社」社員邀約共進晚餐，令小杉放庵喜不自勝。此外，當地赫赫有名的大雅畫廊與裱框店面等，都是他最愛逗留之處，能在這麼獨特的場域吟詩作畫，他深感自己是幸運的，並為此而心懷感激。

春日月滿西湖上
大雅盈溢心懷裡

當他補上最後幾筆素描時，遠方傳來隆隆炮火聲。樹上鳥群四散，炮彈聲響徹天際，幾位僧侶倉惶仰頭望天。在戰火亂世中作畫，使他想起年輕時在日俄之戰中當隨軍畫家的日子。原是晴空萬里的春日好時光，霎時被四面楚歌的黑暗，籠罩大地。

他旅途中的夥伴，沉重悲歎：「我們為何不能和平共處，彼此握手言和呢！」那正是小杉放庵想傳遞的想法。

孫子兵法說「亂而取之」，或許當作者孫武提出「混亂中仍不失機會」的危機策略時，從未把藝術家納入考量，但他應該也能認可，即便身處烽鼓不息的顛沛離散中，仍能描繪寧謐與沉靜之美，或許也能詮釋「亂而取之」之意。顯然，小杉放庵已在風塵之變中，竭盡一切所能了。

（此系列部分內容以小杉放庵的限量作品集為依據，作品集僅印製三百五十冊，畫作是小杉放庵於戰亂期間在中國完成，一九六二年出版。其中第五號版本目前為中國探險學會的典藏書籍。）

二次世界大戰結束七十五年了

SECOND WORLD WAR ENDS
75 YEARS AGO

Cape D'Aguilar, Hong Kong – August 15, 2020

SECOND WORLD WAR ENDS 75 YEARS AGO
Lesson learned?

"JAPAN QUITS!", the full-page headline jumps right out of the newspaper in front of me. This is an actual physical newspaper, not an online digital copy, published on August 15, 1945. The China Lantern was a wartime weekly paper for the U.S. Armed Forces and it had to make an extra printing in the event of Japan surrendering in WWII.

"Dateline Washington, Aug.15," it reads in smaller type at the bottom of the front page, "Japan has officially accepted the Allied terms for unconditional surrender without qualification, Pres. Truman announced last night." In the top corners are pictures of Truman on the left and General Wedemeyer, commander of Allied Forces in the China theater of War, on the right.

On the back page are six large photos with legends. Perhaps most interesting is one of a seized Japanese hospital ship. It is common knowledge that wartime protocol and the Geneva Conventions on code of practice prevented attack on hospitals, including hospital ships and ambulances, usually painted white with a large easily identifiable red cross superimposed.

Writing on end of WWII / 正在寫二次大戰結束的文章

JAP HOSPITAL SHIP SEIZED—This Japanese hospital ship, loaded for routine check-up, was seized by American authorities when found to be carrying machine guns and ammunition in boxes marked "medical supplies," and "patients" who had no wounds beneath bandages, according to Signal Corps caption accompanying this picture received via radio from Manila. Ship was taken to an Allied port for further ex-

Japanese hospital ship seized / 被查獲的日本醫療船

But in this case, the boat was seized by the American authorities when found to be carrying machine guns and ammunition in boxes marked "medical supplies" and with "patients" who had no wounds beneath bandages, according to Signal Corps from Manila. The cargo and 1,500 men were taken to an Allied port. Stealth at war was one of the established tactics of Chinese military strategist Sun Tzu from five centuries BC. The Japanese apparently adopted it well.

Page 7, the entire page, is devoted to summarizing China's eight years of war of resistance against the Japanese with a section on the Japanese war exploitation of Chinese territories. There is also a large picture of Chiang Kai-shek attached. Another picture with caption may well serve today's war mongers, or those putting up such posture and threat toward China. This American military newspaper says, "The Chinese soldier is capable of great endurance and splendid courage which has enabled him to stop the Japanese aggressor time and time again." Many people in the world today should take heed.

My copy of this rare newspaper has a hole in the middle in what looks like it was pierced by a bullet. But, imagined or real, this "defect" perhaps adds to its historic and intrinsic value rather than diminishing it. This piece of

8-pages of newsprint is among the rather large CERS archive of war time documents, newspapers, magazines, pictures and books. Our roomful of WWII aviation history books and artefacts is yet another part of our archive.

Revisiting this archive during the week of the 75th anniversary of Japan's surrender in WWII has more meaning. But the material is so massive that I can only choose a few items to share, including some pieces to show that there were still some lighter reports even during a grim time. Of course, wartime comics and pin-up girls to lift the GI's spirit are not to be neglected also. This inventory below would also demonstrate some of the precious archival material that CERS is holding in its library for future use by select friends and associates.

The materials are original and many are quite frail. Bridging a period of seventy some odd years,

China Lantern Aug 15, 1945 / 《中國燈籠》一九四五年八月十五日

Oct 1945 Young Companion / 一九四五年十月《良友》

they have to be preserved carefully and handled with the greatest care. When going through our archive, I feel not only nostalgic, but also emotional, as if in touch with history. It is very different from reading a replica of such information on a screen in digital form.

For some of the magazines we have a large collection, like the Chinese Young Companion (良友 in Chinese), a pictorial that is modeled after Life Magazine, for which we have a full set of 174 issues. For others we have a few dozen, like Life and Time magazines of the era. Then there are those for which we just have a few sample copies. For example, of the weekly China Lantern we only have four issues, and for the China Command Post, published for the U.S. Armed Forces, we have just one single issue dated February 9, 1945.

But the single issue is already telltale enough, both about heartening news of the European theater of war as well as successes in Asia for the Allied forces as the War was entering its final stages. A full page of pictures shows the

Single issue of Command Post /
《China Command Post》其中一期

Pictures of convoy to Yunnan /
雲南護送之旅的圖片

Full page of comic /
全版面漫畫

CBI Roundup and CB Roundup /
《中緬印戰區新聞綜合報》與
《中緬戰區新聞綜合報》

progress of the first convoy from Burma into China and all the way to its entry into Kunming, a sign of a turning point in the CBI (China Burma India) theater of war. Another full page is devoted to comics, including favorites like Blondie, Dick Tracy and Donald Duck.

Shanghai Evening Post was published in China's wartime capital of Chungking. These small format weekly papers are published on very rough paper with light ink. We have eight issues starting from Dec 24, 1944. The last issue in our collection is from June 17, 1945. On its cover are short dispatches with headlines like, "Wheat Plentiful, Meat Scarce in U.S. This Year", "New Signal School Opened In China", "City Threatened With Cholera" and "OPA Turning Heat On Black Market" (OPA meaning the Office of Price Administration). Biggest section on the front page was devoted to a story headlined "PARTIAL SUFFRAGE FOR CHINA PROMISED WITHIN SIX MONTHS," all in caps.

Our largest collection of newspaper is reserved for two largely similar weekly papers, CBI Roundup and CB Roundup, published in Delhi of India. For the former we have 19 issues from January 14, 1944 to July 12, 1945. For the latter we hold 67 issues, a few of which are double copies of the same issue. They are dated from March 9, 1944 to September 27, 1945, over a month beyond the final surrender of the Japanese.

The issue on Aug 16, 1945, a day after Japan's surrender, besides announcing "President Truman Reports Japs Accept Allied Terms; MacArthur Supreme Head" also offers a subhead - "Emperor Will Be Subject To Order Of Commander," certainly a huge humiliation for the defeated Japanese. A sidebar story on the front page also features "U.S. Sole Owner Of Atomic Bomb Manufacturing" offering in the following pages 10 and 11 pictures and more details concerning the atomic bomb.

The story actually falls on Page 8 with multiple short stories, one with a photograph of the Oak Ridge, Tennessee plant where the atomic bomb was made. Another story is headlined "Lasting Effects Of Bomb Denied." Yet two others have the headlines "U.S. Committee To Plan Atomic Energy Control" and "Uranium Ore In Explosive". A small story on the same page attests to "Late President Aware Of Bomb Potentiality" referring to President Roosevelt before his passing away. One dispatch, titled "Developers Identified," is dedicated to three American scientists who played a leading part in the Bomb's development. They are Dr. Robert Oppenheimer, "a genius and inspiration" as noted by Secretary of War

Pictures of Dec 7, 1941 Pearl Harbor / 珍珠港攝於一九四一年十二月七日
Battle of HK and British forces prisoners / 於香港的戰爭與英軍戰俘
Occupation of HK by Japan / 日本佔領香港

Henry Stimson, Dr. Ernest Lawrence, inventor of the atom-smashing cyclotron, and Dr. Richard Tolman.

Among magazines in the CERS collection, Time and Life are familiar to many and would not require much description except that we hold some of the most crucial issues related to WWII. One collection however is worthy of note due to it being little-known. Yank is a pictorial magazine published by the American military mainly for its serviceman during the War.

It comes in a format similar to Life though with fewer pages (24), and the stories are generally simpler. As one can imagine, most of the infantry and fighting forces who were its intended readers were young and not fully educated adults. Nonetheless, the magazine holds some very important War images and stories. An example is our last issue, from Dec. 14, 1945, four months after the end of the War. The cover is of US army and navy servicemen crowding to make their Christmas purchase at the newly opened PX store in Tokyo. Inside the issue there are stories about the G.I. Bill for sending veterans to college. A story about job seeking opportunities takes up three full pages, and there is a page with pictures from occupied Japan.

The issue on Oct. 5, 1945 has a cover of the Japanese signing their surrender papers on board the battleship USS Missouri, with an inside spread of General MacArthur signing on behalf of the U.S., plus a copy of the signed document. A long multiple-page story describes "3 BEATEN CITIES", namely Nagasaki, Tokyo and Hiroshima.

Our Chinese monthly magazine of note is a pictorial with the title of Young Companion. Of the full set of 174 issues covering 1926 to 1945 (four years from 1941 to 1945 being disrupted without printing) Issue 172 of October 1945 is notable for being published at the ending of the War. This issue is unique in not only being the resumption of publishing of the journal, but also in celebrating China's first National Day of October 10 after the Japanese surrender. Besides having the portrait of Chiang Kai-shek on the cover what is perhaps most significant is that the five major victorious national flags are included at the bottom, that of China, America, Britain, France and the Soviet Union. As a pictorial magazine, many of the photographs are important documentation of China over two turbulent decades of change.

Another rare addition to our collection is the Japanese wartime magazine History Pictorial（歷史寫真）of which we have three issues, and Pictorial Weekly（寫真週報）spanning 1938 to 1944, of which we have 17 issues. Of particular interest to me is Issue 202 of January 7, 1942. Though barely two weeks after Hong Kong's surrender to the Japanese on Christmas Day, the magazine, besides having a major story on the attack at Pearl Harbor of December 7, also includes the fall of Hong Kong with a double spread. It was to be followed with another spread of pictures taken during the occupation of Hong Kong, in Issue 208 of February 28, 1942.

War is never pleasant and always brutal and sad. At the end there is no winner, not even for the "victorious". But history repeats itself as battle after battle and war after war is waged. Our archive of WWII perhaps will give a bit of rare record for whoever is not only interested in history of a war that ended 75 years ago, but also in a lesson to future generation to avoid going to war, despite whatever differences or ambitions we may have.

二次世界大戰結束七十五年了 引以為鑒？

「日本全面放棄！」報紙上頭條新聞以全版大字，出現我眼前。這是一九四五年八月十五日出刊的實體報紙，而非網媒電子報。《中國燈籠》(The China Lantern) 是世界大戰期間，專印製出刊給美國軍方看的週報，隨著日本於二戰期間宣佈投降，消息一出，週報得超量加印號外才滿足得了搶閱的讀者。

頭版底部有小字印刷，標示報紙日期：「華盛頓，八月十五日」；緊接著是一行文字：「杜魯門 (Truman) 總統昨晚對外宣稱，日本已正式接受同盟國條約，全面無條件投降。」頁面頂端角落刊了幾張照片，左邊那張是杜魯門右邊是二戰期間被派往中國的同盟國將領魏德邁 (Wedemeyer)。

背頁則是醒目的六張大圖與圖說。其中最引人注目的，或許是一張被同盟國查獲的日本醫療船。根據戰爭協議與「日內瓦公約」的明文規定，大家普遍認同，任何大動干戈的交火攻擊，都應避開醫院，包括醫療船與救護車——它們的外觀一般都塗上白底套上紅十字——一個非常易於辨識的標誌。

但這艘被美國當局攔下的日本醫療船，根據駐馬尼拉的陸軍通信兵團資料顯示，裝載的卻是機關槍與一箱箱的彈藥，只不過，箱子外的標示，卻是「醫療補給」，以及一

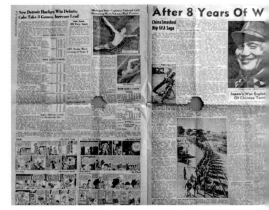

批評開繃帶不見任何傷口的「病患者」。於是，這艘被攔下的貨船與一千五百名壯丁被帶往同盟國的港口。「故形兵之極、至於無形。」，是公元前五世紀中國孫子兵法的戰術之一；顯然日本照單全收，實踐得很徹底。

週報的第七頁，通篇內容都處理與總結中國對抗日本的八年抗戰，其中一部分則敘述日本在中國領土上各種剝削與殺戮行跡。此外，還有一張蔣介石的照片也附於其上。另一張附有圖說的照片，今天各地發動戰爭的始作俑者，或那些挑釁與威脅中國的對象看在眼裡，可引以為鑒。這份美國軍事報紙寫道：「中國士兵的堅持不懈、奮勇應戰，一次次頑抗阻絕日本侵略者。」暮鼓晨鐘，也是今日世人該聽進去的一句話。

我手上這份稀有的報紙，中間有個洞，像極了被子彈貫穿的破口。不管這破洞是想像或真相，如此突兀的「缺陷」，其實，更增添這份舊報的歷史感與價值。這份總計八頁的新聞週報，是中國探險學會頗具規模得戰時記錄典藏的其中一份檔案，其他藏品還包括報紙、雜誌、畫作與書籍。此外，我們的檔案庫裡還有許多二

Report on Japan's surrender / 有關日本投降的報道
End of War in Chungking paper / 重慶報章刊登戰事結束的消息

Covers of Yank magazine / 《Yank》雜誌封面

戰期間的航空歷史書籍與相關文物。

在「日本二戰期間投降七十五週年」這一週重讀相關檔案，意義非凡。只是，資料多而龐雜，我只能挑一些來分享，包括一些小品，讓人知道即便在風聲鶴唳的艱困年代，仍不乏一些輕鬆詼諧的報導。當然，戰時的漫畫與提振美軍士氣的海報女郎，是不可或缺的題材之一。以下說明的內容，將把中國探險學會這段期間蒐集的珍貴檔案，與讀者分享，這些資料將來也會讓一些重要朋友與夥伴作展示之用。

這些資料都是原件，大部分已殘破不堪；歷經七十多年歲月的洗滌，它們需要被妥善保管，小心存取。每每翻閱這些檔案，我忍不住感時撫事，一時仿若與歷史搭上線，情緒有些波動。這種感覺與閱讀熒幕上電子版本的複製品，迥然有別。

我們典藏的雜誌還不少。以仿效美國老牌周刊《生活》(Life) 為主的畫報《良友》中文版期刊，我們共蒐集了一百七十四期；而當年的《生活》與《時代》(Time) 雜誌，我們也有數十期份數。有些雜誌我們僅有幾份樣本，譬如《中國燈籠》週報，我們只有四份；另外為美國軍方而設的《China Command Post》，我們只有一份，標示的出刊日期為一九四五年二月九日。

但即便只有一期單份，已具足話題性，內容含括振奮人心的歐洲戰場，以及同盟國軍方在二戰後期，於亞洲地區旗開得勝的消息。此外，全版的照片也標示從緬甸入中國再一路抵達昆明的首批護送軍力與進度，那是中緬印戰役的轉折點。另一頁則被美國人熱愛的經典漫畫，佔據全版面，包括白朗黛 (Blondie)、狄克‧崔西 (Dick Tracy) 與唐老鴨 (Donald Duck)。

《大美晚報》(Shanghai Evening Post) 在中國抗日期間的首都重慶發行。這份格式較小的週報，紙張粗糙，印刷刻印的顏色也淺淡。我們共蒐集了從一九四四年十二月二十四日開始出刊的八份期數，最後一份的日期，是一九四五年的六月十七日。這一期的封面處理了幾則新聞，標題分別是：「美國今年麵粉足夠，肉類不足」、「新通信學校即將於中國成立」、「飽受霍亂威脅之城」、「物價管理局對黑市施壓」；而頭版最大的篇幅，下了這樣的標題：「開放中國部分選舉權，允諾半年內執行」。

我們蒐集到最大的報紙，是兩大屬性相似的週報，其一是《中緬印戰區新聞綜合報》(CBI Roundup)，另一則是《中緬戰區新聞綜合報》(CB Roundup)，兩份的發行地點都在印度的德里。第一份綜合報，我們總共蒐集了十九份，從一九四四年一月十四日至一九四五年七月十二日；而第二份綜合報則有六十七份，其中有幾份重複、屬同一期，出刊日期從一九四四年三月九日至

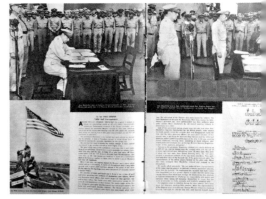

Japan surrenders on USS Missouri /
日本在美國軍艦「密蘇里號」簽署投降文書
Bombing of Nagasaki etc / 轟炸長崎和其他城市

一九四五年九月二十七日，那是日本投降後一個月的事了。

一九四五年八月十六日出刊的那一期，正值日本投降隔天，報紙斗大的標題，昭告天下：「杜魯門總統宣稱日本接受同盟國條約，麥克阿瑟接任盟軍總司令」，下方副標一行字寫道：「天皇將服從指揮官命令」，那簡直是對戰敗國日本的奇恥大辱。頭版邊欄一則新聞以「美國獨家生產製造原子彈」為題，並在第十與十一頁接續報導更多與原子彈相關的圖片與細節等說明。

有關原子彈的內容，其實搭配了幾則小故事，在第八頁中出現——當時的原子彈就在田納西州的橡樹嶺 (Oak Ridge) 實驗室研製。另一則故事以大標題寫道：「否認原子彈的永久傷害」，而另外兩則標題，分別是：「美國委員會計劃原子能管制」與「鈾礦石在炸藥中的應用」。另外在同一頁的一則小故事，則證實了羅斯福總統離世前的隱憂：「已故總統警覺原子彈威力」。還有一則以「研發者已確認」為題的新聞報導，表達對三位美國科學家在原子彈研發過程中的領導性角色——被美國戰爭部長亨利.史汀生形容為「天才與啟發者」的原子彈之父羅伯特·歐本海默 (Robert Oppenheimer) 博士、歐內斯特.勞倫斯 (Ernest Lawrence) 博士，以及理察·托爾曼 (Richard Tolman) 博士。

在中國探險學會所蒐集的雜誌中，《時代》與《生活》是大家耳熟能詳的刊物，不需我在此多贅述，值得留意的是我們珍藏了有關二戰報導至為重要的期數。不過，其中一份蒐藏因為它鮮為人知而顯得特殊，那是《Yank》雜誌，屬畫報雜誌，由美國軍方出版發行，主要讀者是二戰期間的軍人。

《Yank》的格式、風格，與《生活》雜誌相近，只是頁數比較少，只有二十四頁，故事內容普遍淺顯易懂，原因不難想像，因為佔主要讀者群的步兵與戰鬥部隊隊員中，大多是年輕人，與未受完整教育的成人。即便如此，《Yank》也不乏一些重要的戰爭圖片與報導。舉個例子，我們蒐藏的最後一期《Yank》雜誌，出刊日期為一九四五年十二月十四日，當時已是二戰結束的四個月後。封面是美國陸軍與海軍軍人，湧向新開幕的東京軍人福利社進行聖誕大採購。內文則報導了幾則與「美國軍人權利法案」(G.I. Bill) 相關的故事，在法案保障下，許多退役軍人紛紛到大學進修，完成學業。另外還有工作招募的報導，也佔了三大版面；另一頁則是戰敗國日本的照片。

而一九四五年十月五日出刊那一期的封面故事，是日本代表團在美國軍艦「密蘇里號」簽署《降伏文書》，正式完成無條件投降儀式；內文還以跨頁照片刊載麥克阿瑟總司令代表美方簽署文件，並附上雙方簽署的投降文件，佐圖為證。然後是好幾頁長篇大論的報導，敘述「三大被重擊城市」——長崎、東京與廣島。

我們認為值得留意的中國月刊，是名為《良友》的畫報。全套一百七十四期，從一九二六年到一九四五年出刊都完整蒐藏起來（從一九四一年至一九四五年長達四年期間因戰受阻而停刊。）其中一九四五年十月出刊的一百七十二期，因為在二戰結束後發

Report on atomic bomb / 有關原子彈的報道

行，而備受矚目——除了復刊這件事比較特別，中國在日本投降後首次歡度雙十國慶也是非同尋常的亮點。此時的封面大圖，想當然爾是蔣介石，但最意義不凡的，或許是封面底部以勝利之姿隨風搖曳的五國國旗——中國、美國、英國、法國與當時的蘇聯。若以畫報的標準而言，當時的許多攝影師，其實都肩負重任，他們以鏡頭記錄了這段二十多年來最動盪不安與風雲變色的中國實況。

另外值得一提的罕見蒐藏，是日戰期間日本軍方出版的雜誌《歷史寫真》，我們總共有三份；而《寫真週報》則蒐集了十四份，出刊年份從一九三八年至一九四二年間。其中我特別感興趣的是一九四二年一月七日出刊的第二零二期——兩週前香港才在聖誕節當天向日軍投降，同一份雜誌以跨兩頁的版面，來處理發生於十二月七日「偷襲珍珠港」的主題報導，同時含括香港的失守。後續在一九四二年二月二十八日的第二零八期，再以跨頁的圖片刊載香港被日軍佔領的報導。

戰爭永遠與快樂沾不上邊，從來就是殘酷無情、令人痛心疾首的；最終也從未有真正的贏家，所謂「獲勝一方」都只是虛張聲勢而已。但歷史不斷重蹈覆轍，一波波的戰火與煙硝彈雨，從未停歇。我們蒐集的二戰文史資料提供了一些罕見的記錄，不但對有意鑽研七十五年前那段戰爭歷史的人，有所助益，對未來的下一代更是寶貴的教訓——無論我們有多大的差異、有多大的野心，都要竭盡所能地遠離戰爭。

1938-39 Japan military magazines / 一九三八年至一九三九年日本軍事雜誌

1941-45 Japan military magazines / 一九四一年至一九四五年日本軍事雜誌

最
後
的
舢
舨

THE LAST WOODEN SAMPAN

Cape D'Aguilar, Hong Kong
– January 28, 2021

THE LAST WOODEN SAMPAN

There is a short street in the heart of Wan Chai, Hong Kong's busiest district. Simple as the street sign is, its name, Sam Pan Street, is highly significant. It relates to the passing of something historical and unique for centuries, perhaps not only for Hong Kong, but also for much of coastal China.

Sam Pan literally means "three boards". The most primitive and simple specimen was likely made from three pieces of wood joined together. Over time, the two Chinese characters "three boards" (三 板) were replaced by (舢舨), phonetically equivalent yet becoming more elegant and descriptive with addition of the character for boat (舟) to the left of both words. In fact, the word is derived from a hieroglyph of two internal boards or two persons with a single long oar on an enclosed three sided vehicle.

Sam Pan Street (三板街) is an old street, once famous, or infamous, for its brothels. It used to sit just a couple blocks from the waterfront in Wan Chai, probably near where sampans anchored. Today, despite the landfill that has taken the shoreline outward for hundreds of meters, the ancient street still retains the more original and ancient name, though no sampans or brothels are to be found there. *This is important evidence regarding the derivation of Chinese words and Hong Kong's geography along Victoria Harbor, as well as the evolution and fate of the sampan boat.*

What is most significant about a sampan is that it is not a traditional Western row boat. It is a yuloh（搖櫓）boat and that word is almost synonymous with the word sampan. Yuloh means the boat has a single sculling oar pivoting in the rear and is propelled along by a left and right, or push and pull, alternating action of the arms with a certain rhythm. An even back and forth yuloh motion would take the boat forward. An uneven pace and force would turn the boat to one direction or the other at will, of course only for the experienced. Sculling with a single oar is best done while in a standing position, though at times it can be conducted while seated if a more leisurely pace is desired in calm water.

For hundreds of years, perhaps even over a thousand years, the yulou operated sampan was a must-have for coastal transport or river channel ferrying over water. Even on a much larger fishing, cargo or military junk,

舟 zhōu

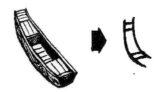

这是一个象形字，像一只弯弯的小船，船上还有横木，十分逼真。本义是"船"。汉字中有"舟"旁的字，大多与船有关。

Sam Pan Street today / 今天的三板街
Evolution of word "boat" / 舟字的演變

Dong Yuan Xiaoxiang painting / 董源畫作《瀟湘圖》
Detail of yuloh in painting / 畫作中搖櫓的細節

the sampan was essential and ubiquitous, acting as a tender from boat to shore. Such boats were not only popular in China, but worked their way across the ocean to Japan, as well as throughout Southeast Asia.

Chinese paintings from earlier dynasties often depict sampans or junks with yuloh in their scenes. Dong Yuan (董源 934 – 962 AD) of the Five Dynasties depicted in his Xiaoxiang (瀟湘圖) landscape, now held by the Palace Museum in Beijing, a sampan with a standing yulou oarsman. One of the most famous scroll paintings, "Along the River During Qingming Festival" (清明上河圖) from the Northern Song Dynasty by Zhang Zeduan (張澤端 1085-1145), showed the stern section of a boat, with several men maneuvering a large yuloh oar. An entire genre of Chinese landscape artists often included a small sampan boat with a yuloh oarsman.

Perhaps the most renowned Japanese print making artist Hokusai (1760-1849) from the mid-19th century depicted yulou on a sampan in many of his art pieces, including among the famous Mount Fuji series. His work has now become decorative art found in many homes and on much consumer merchandise, though most people may not have noticed his inclusion of the sampan in his art. Another print making master Hiroshige (1797-1858), a contemporary of Hokusai, also depicted yuloh sampan in many of his work. A well-known 20th Century artist Hoan Kosugi (1881-1964) likewise decorated his lower Yangtze landscape masterpieces with boats and yuloh rowers.

Western scholars have made much mention and even detailed study of the Chinese sampan. Joseph Needham's seminal work Science and Civilization in China devoted an entire section to Chinese nautical science and described the use of the traditional sampan. A huge volume published by the U.S. Naval Institute at Annapolis "Junks and Sampans of the Yangtze "provided many detailed drawings of all types of sampans along the Yangtze.

A very posh volume, The Sampans from Canton, with ninety-six detailed drawings, was published by a distinguished foundation in Sweden, after protracted litigations in court to prohibit the collection from leaving the country despite being auctioned off. Yet another book, prepared and published in China with selections from a collection of old photos at the Royal Museums at Greenwich "Sampan Girl Smiles" documented junks and

Hokusai Ferry boat Ryogoku Bridge /
葛飾北齋畫作《御廄川岸見兩國橋夕陽》

Hiroshige prints with yuloh boats /
歌川廣重的作品含括搖櫓舢舨

Kosugi yuloh boat lower Yangtze /
小杉放庵的江南山水畫出現搖櫓掌船

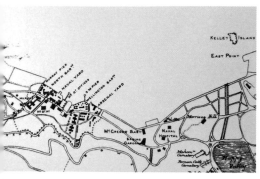

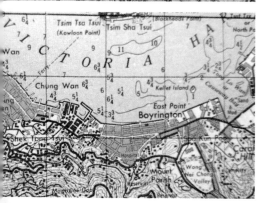

Wan Chai map 1845 / 一八四五年灣仔地圖
Wan Chai map 1905 / 一九零五年灣仔地圖
Wan Chai map 1949 after landfill /
一九四九年填海後的灣仔地圖

sampans along the China coast within recent memory. Such materials are evidence of the importance of the sampan even in the eyes of western artists and scholars.

However, back home where the sampan originated, we are witnessing the eclipse of this age-old heritage and craftsmanship, disappearing without much concern or notice. Within the last thirty to forty years, the traditional wooden sampan in Hong Kong has all but disappeared. The same is probably true for the rest of Asia. What I saw in the 1970s of wooden Yuloh boats on the Li River in Guilin have long become obsolete. In part, they were replaced by motorized small boats. In other instances, shortage of wood and advance of substitute material and technology brought about the advent of the fiberglass sampan; lighter, easier to construct with a mould, and thus costing much less.

In early summer of 2020, due in part to the pandemic restricting our people from moving around, all CERS staff started working closely with their immediate communities, as long as their activities abided by respective government's regulations at the time. Likewise, in Hong Kong, we have chosen to start new projects in nearby Lantau Island, a piece of land larger than Hong Kong Island itself, yet with much more pristine area and sparser population. One of the locations we focused on is Tai O, once an important *fishing village of Hong Kong up until perhaps forty years ago.*

Tai O used to be home to over 30,000 inhabitants, mainly fishing families. But over the years its population has decreased to around 3,000 as younger people sought work in the city. Left behind are mainly senior members of family, generally retired and of advanced age, many living in stilt houses over water. Young people are now few except for those who prefer a quiet and more leisurely life.

One such small group we befriended has formed an association to preserve their own history and cultural heritage, that of the fishing community of Tai O. Among key members of the association, we quickly became close friends of Timmy, a cafe owner, and Chi Chuen, an artist. It has been their long-time wish to find a wooden sampan as a specimen for preservation, and to use it to teach the younger generation the art of yuloh.

We came at the right time, and I took it upon myself to help source a wooden sampan. Soon I realized it was a

Kundien log used in 1920 / 一九二零年的坤甸木材

Sam Pan Street 1920 / 一九二零年三板街

hopeless proposition. We asked at the remaining three most important fishing communities of Hong Kong, Aberdeen, Shau Kei Wan and Cheung Chau. Everywhere we asked, we hit a stone wall. "Are you kidding, they are long gone." "Sure, you find me one and I buy it," came the answers. Even the Maritime Museum has long been looking for one with no prospect in sight. But CERS never gives up, even in the face of adversity.

Though for decades I am used to explore with my fleet of cars and even our own exploration boats, launching expeditions from our multiple centers and bases, now I have to go to Lantau by ferry and Tai O by bus.

While searching through the internet, I came upon a newspaper article from 2016. It is about an older sampan lady who was then 74. "Mui Jei" (Little sister Big sister) lives in Saikung, a town in the eastern outskirts of Hong Kong with a typhoon shelter. This over the years has become the mooring for a couple hundred pleasure boats and small fishing boats. With this base, some of the old-time shipyards also managed to survive. The area has also become a popular weekend hang-out for enjoying water sports and seafood restaurants. The focus of the 2016 newspaper article was about Mui Jei being the owner of the last wooden sampan.

Through friends who often go to Saikung, we soon located Mui Jei and befriended her. Over the next few weeks, I was to find myself making multiple trips to Saikung. Xavier, our filmmaker, also made several rounds as we interviewed Mui Jei to film her story. Astor, our anthropologist, also came to help make the story more organized and comprehensive. We even brought student interns along to observe on the side. Mui Jei's husband, now 84 years old, drove his motorized wooden ferry plying us back and forth, following the calm and quiet wake of his wife's paddling in her sampan.

However, Mui Jei has no desire to get rid of her lovely sampan, something she has cared for like her own child. The sampan was given to her by her aunt almost thirty years ago, though it was first built and registered in 1976. For over twenty years she has managed her sampan with extreme care. Ferrying weekend tourists has been her pastime as well as providing a small stipend after her retirement.

"Many people have asked, even movie groups have offered to purchase my boat," said Mui Jei. "But my answer is always no," she said. Her stories span her childhood as a girl of a fishing family through decades to today. About a year ago, she had a medical surgery and since then could not continue to row her sampan as her trade at senior age. The sampan had been kept under tight canvas and heavy plastic wrap for over a year when we met her.

As we became better acquainted over a period of time, I told Mui Jei about our preservation work over the years. We even brought a 90-year-old boat-builder to meet her, after which he explained to us all the intricacies and craftsmanship of a wooden boat. Fan Kwei Sen told us about the special kundien wood from Borneo Indonesia that must be used for the most critical parts of a boat, like the keel and the stern. This heavy dense wood, if dropped into water, would sink faster than a stone. This is the same kind of wood that supports the stilt houses in Tai O.

My patience and charm must have paid off. As if just being curious, I asked Mui Jei how much she would ultimately sell her boat for. "That's no one's business, I can give it away if I wish," came her answer. That seemed like a perfect line for me to catch on. Thus, our chase, or purchase, came to an end as we negotiated this "give-away" per se of a priceless piece, the last wooden sampan of Hong Kong.

We named the sampan Mui Jei Gor, related to her and her husband as a big brother. Today Mui Jei Gor sits quietly gracing the façade of the stilt terrace of Timmy's Solo Café in Tai O. It is now cared for by two friends of the Tai O Cultural Preservation Association, and admired by many who come along to experience the flavor of an old fishing village. It also serves occasional duty as not just a specimen, but for young students to learn the art of yulou.

While Mui Jei is soon turning 80, I start imagining that Mui Jei Gor can still reproduce at age 45, cloning itself through 3D printing, or making a mould for fiberglass replicas. As many Hong Kong youths are turning to western style kayaking, why not go retro and popularize Yuloh sampan. Perhaps soon we can even organize in Tai O a Yuloh competition or a festival. CERS has created a very successful Crossbow Festival for the Lisu hilltribe in Yunnan. I cannot see why a parallel festival in Hong Kong cannot be designed and implemented.

The pandemic may have kept me home, but we managed to produce some tangible value during this trying time, by salvaging this last relic of a long historic past. It has become my great pleasure that, when on an occasional outing on this sampan, neighbors among the stilt houses along the shore would yell over, "Where did you manage to get this old boat?" And I would yell back my answer, "From Tao Bao on the internet."

Tai O Lantau stilt houses / 大嶼山大澳的高腳屋

Yuloh sampan in Shanghai / 上海的搖櫓舢舨
Yuloh oars Li River Guilin 1970s /
七十年代桂林灘江上的木頭搖櫓船

經常出現搖櫓的舢舨小船，其中包括遠近馳名的富士山系列作品集。他的這些代表作深入許多家庭與消費品的佈置藝術，儘管大部分人並未注意到這些藝術創作裡的舢舨符號。另一位與葛飾北齋同時代的日本浮世繪畫家，歌川廣重（一七九七年至一八五八年），也喜歡把搖櫓舢舨的圖象含括在他的作品中；而二十世紀畫家小杉放庵（一八八一年至一九六二年）同樣對搖櫓掌船的元素情有獨鍾，並繪入他的中國江南山水畫裡。

西方學者提出許多與中國舢舨相關的論述，也對此深入研究。李約瑟的重量級著作《中國科學與文明》(Science and Civilization in China) 以一整個篇章來處理中國航海的科學，並詳盡敘述傳統舢舨的用途。美國海軍學院出版的大書《長江之帆船與舢舨》(Junks and Sampans of the Yangtze)，對航行於長江流域的各種舢舨，提供許多具體的圖示說明。

瑞典著名基金會曾出版《來自廣州的舢舨》(The Sampans from Canton) 一書，書中繪製了九十六幅與舢舨相關的畫，精美細緻；這本書歷經拖延再三的法庭訴訟，雖然最終拍板定案，藏畫不得帶離瑞典，但最終仍被拍賣。還有值得一提的另一本在中國籌劃與出版的書籍，內容是從格林威治皇家博物館蒐集而得的一批老照片《舢舨女孩的微笑》(Sampan Girl Smiles)，其中記錄了近期航行於中國沿海一帶的帆船與舢舨。這些都是與舢舨相關的重要資

訊與證據，即便在西方藝術家與學者眼中，都是彌足珍貴的史料。

雖然如此，回到舢舨的發源地，我們卻見證這個充滿歷史感的寶藏與技藝，逐漸在生活中黯然隱退，甚至乏人問津。過去三十至四十年來，香港的傳統木舢舨都已全數消失；我想在其他亞洲國家，舢舨大概也都銷聲匿跡了。如今回想，我在桂林的灕江上看過的木頭搖櫓船，已成歷史一絕，往後再也見不到。有些地方，其實是將傳統小船改裝成摩托船；另外一些狀況則要歸因於木料短缺，外加較先進的替代材質與技術的引進，玻璃纖維舢舨於焉問世；這類船隻按模具開發，不但更易於製造，重量也更輕，成本自然更低。

二零二零年初夏，因疫情禁令，中國探險學會員工無法如往常般，不能隨心所欲地外出行動，我們員工在不觸犯各別政府的法令前提下，開始與周邊社區建立緊密的合作關係。在香港亦然；我們選擇在鄰近的大嶼山——一個比香港本島面積更大、人口更少卻保有更多未開發地區的島嶼，展開新計劃。這項計劃的其中一個焦點，是近四十年前曾為香港重要漁村的大澳。

早些年，大澳逾三萬居民中，大部分是捕魚人家；但近幾年來，以年輕人為主的族群急速外移至城裡工作，人口降至三千左右，大部分是家中退休的長輩與高齡老者，大多仍居住於鐵皮高腳屋。除

Chi Chuen's panarama drawing of Tai O as of 1988 / 志泉繪畫一九八八年的大澳全景圖

了一些比較想慢活與嚮往過悠閒日子的年輕人以外，島上幾乎不見其他青壯年身影。我們的學會，認識了一群人，這小團體積極著手成立協會，想藉此保護屬於大澳漁民社群的歷史與文化遺產。我們很快就與協會其中兩位核心成員——咖啡館老闆添明與藝術家志泉，成為好朋友。他們長久以來不斷尋尋覓覓，想蒐藏一艘木製舢舨當歷史文物，以此當搖櫓藝術的教材，教育年輕下一代。

一切來得正是時候，我自告奮勇協助他們尋找木舢舨的資源。但我很快就發現，這根本是徒勞無功的不可能任務。我詢問香港仔、筲箕灣與長洲這三個僅存的香港重要漁村，每問一次，便碰一鼻子灰，真令人洩氣——「你在開什麼玩笑啊，這些東西早就不存在了。」有些人還回應：「你若能幫我找到一艘，我也買下來。」其實就連香港海事博物館也苦尋舢舨很久，至今仍渺無影蹤。儘管海底撈月，中國探險學會也不輕言放棄。

雖然數十年來，我早已習慣以我們的車隊，甚至是我們自己的探險船上山下海，也從各個不同中心點與基地出發，展開長途遠征，但現在，我得搭渡輪到大嶼山，再搭巴士到大澳。

透過網路搜尋，我找到一篇二零一六年的報章撰文，內文提及一位當年七十四歲的舢舨老婦「妹姐」；住在香港東邊外圍市郊、設有颱風庇護港的西貢。過去幾年來，此地已成為好一些遊艇與小漁船停靠之處；由於船舶航行頻繁，這據點自然也保有一些舊時代的船廠；此外，這區域最為人津津樂道的，便是週末水上活動與海鮮餐廳。那份二零一六年的舊報文章，記錄了妹姐是最後一艘木舢舨的船主。

透過經常往返西貢的朋友相助，我們很快便找到妹姐，並與她結交成朋友。接下來幾週，我去了好幾趟西貢，而團隊的影片製作人李伯達 (Xavier) 在我們採訪妹姐時，還特別拍下她的故事；我們團隊中的人類學家黃雅儀 (Astor) 也協助將妹姐的故事結構，處理得更流暢、更全面與詳盡。我們甚至讓實習生隨行，在一旁觀察學習。妹姐的丈夫，今年八十四歲，經常開著那台機動木渡船，不辭辛勞地把我們載進載出，緊跟在妻子那艘「重出江湖」、沉靜無聲的搖櫓舢舨身後。

然而，妹姐把那艘舢舨視如己出，就像長久呵護照顧的自家孩子般，捨不得割讓或出售。雖然這是阿嫂三十年前送她的禮物，但這艘舢舨最初是在一九七六年打造與註冊。二十多年來，妹姐對她的舢舨照顧得無微不至；從前每個週末搖櫓載客渡海的記憶，是她忘不了的舊時光，這份工作也為她積攢了一筆退休後的養老金。

「很多人問過我，還有電影公司也來出價，要買我的船，」妹姐繼續說道：「但我的答案永遠一樣，『不賣』。」她的人生故事從童年的漁家小姑娘到搖櫓渡海的長者；一年前接受手術治療後，自此便無法再以高齡之姿繼續她的搖櫓事業。當我們與她會面時，這艘舢舨已被收藏起來超過一年，以帆布與厚重的塑膠袋層層包覆起來。

經過一段時間的互動，我們越來越熟悉，我告訴妹姐我們這幾年的保育工作；我們甚至請來一位九十歲的資深造船工作者樊桂森來見她。父親為他名字加這麼多木，便是希望他繼承五代造木船之祖業。他為我們講解打造一艘木船，涉及什麼樣錯綜複雜的工程與技藝。樊先生名字有六個木字，難怪擅於製造木船，他還告訴我們，木船最講究的部分，譬如船的龍骨與尾部，必須要使用印尼婆羅洲較特別的坤甸木。這些高密度的木頭，一旦落海會沉得比石頭還快；在大澳漁村的水上人家蓋的高腳房子，用的也是這種木頭。

Boatbuilder Fan with Mui Jei /
造船工作者樊先生與妹姐

我鐵杵磨針的耐性與個人魅力，終於開花結果。我以一種好奇的口吻向妹姐探詢，如果要出售這艘舢舨，她心中最終的價格會是多少。她回答：「那不是做生意，只要我願意，我甚至可以無價捐贈出去。」我見機不可失，乘勝追擊；於是乎，我們之間的一來一往或採購洽談，最終陪伴定案——妹姐決定差不多是「捐贈」這艘無價的船隻——香港最後的木舢舨。

我們將舢舨命名為「妹姐哥」，記念主人妹姐與她的丈夫大哥。今天，「妹姐哥」被安置於添明的蘇廬咖啡店，平靜優雅地停靠在大澳水上人家的高腳屋門面。這艘歷史感的舢舨現在由「文化保護協會」的兩位朋友看管，讓無數前來體驗老漁村風貌的人，多了一份真實感。但這艘舢舨並非只是靜態文物，偶爾一些時候，我們也會把它推出海中，讓年輕學生實際學習搖櫓的藝術。

妹姐轉瞬八十歲了，我開始想像已屆四十五歲的「妹姐哥」，是否可藉由 3D 列印來複製與重製，或做個模具，以玻璃纖維的材質來打造另一艘「妹姐哥」。尤其現在，香港年輕人熱衷西式獨木舟，何不「見風轉舵」，把握良機讓搖櫓舢舨再度風生水起，復興搖櫓文化。也許不久的將來，我們可以在大澳舉辦搖櫓競賽或相關的節慶活動。中國探險學會曾在中國雲南為傈僳族人舉辦過弩弓節，成效卓著。在香港，類似的活動籌劃與想法，我找不到任何難以落實的理由。

全球疫情或許使我「坐困圍城」，但為了搶救這份幾乎要被歷史洪流淹沒的最後一塊瑰寶，並重新賦予它生命力，我們在這段嘗試階段仍竭力發想各種實際可行、值得一試的計劃。閒來無事時，我最大的樂趣便是跳上舢舨，搖櫓外出。高腳房的社區鄰里見狀，都愛站在岸邊高聲叫喚：「你從哪裡弄到這艘舊船啊？」我不厭其煩回答：「網路上淘寶啦……」。

Stilt houses on Kundien wood support / 高腳屋以坤甸木作支柱

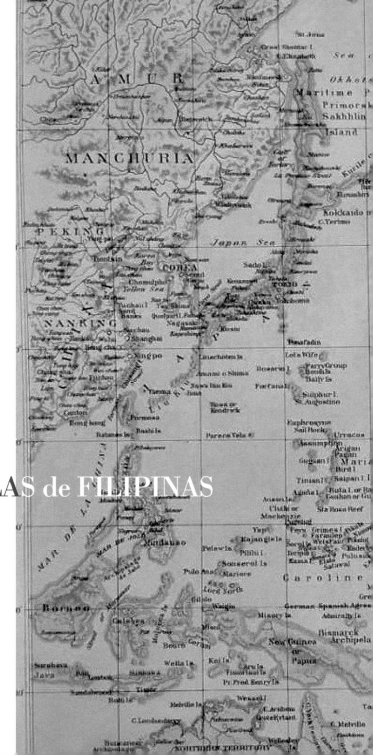

菲
律
賓
地
圖
集
的
推
論

COROLLARY TO ATLAS de FILIPINAS

Hong Kong – January 16, 2021

Bering Sea

Pribilof Islands

St. Paul

Commander Is.

Near Islands

Andreanof Is.

Queen Charlotte Isd.

CALIFORN

Equatorial Scale

0   500   1000   1500   2000   2500   3000   3500   4000   4500   5000 K.

Rock

Shoal

Midway Is.

Pearl Hermes Reef

Maro Reef

Gardner I.

Brooks Shoal

Necker I.

Bird I.

HAWAIIAN

Honolulu

Oahu   Molokai

Maui

Hawaii

ISLANDS

Island

No 1

Wake I.

Taongi I.

Marshall Islands

Schjetman Reef

Johnston I.

ISLAS FILIPINAS

ihs

PACIFICO

OBSERVATORIO DE MANILA

Shoal

Singano Shoal

Palmyra I.

Baldew Reef

Diana Shoal

Washington or New York I.

Fanning Is.

Gilbert Islands

Makin Island

Howland I.

Christmas I.

Jarvis I.

Phoenix Islands

Canton

McKean I.

Birnie I.

Enderbury I.

Gardner I.

Hull I.

Phoenix I.

Sydney I.

Malden I.

Starbuck I.

Marquesas Islands

Nukahiva

Ellice Islands

Solomon Islands

Santa Cruz Islands

Union Group

Victoria I.

Duboisl

Tongareva

Caroline Atoll

Society Islands

New Hebrides

SAMOAN IS.

Suvarof Is.

Low Archipelago or Paumota

Tahiti

FIJI IS.

COROLLARY TO ATLAS *de* FILIPINAS

The title is telling enough. Though published by the U.S. Coast and Geodetic Survey of the Treasury Department in 1900 and printed by the government printing office in Washington, the cover embossed in gold color reads "ATLAS de FILIPINAS" in Spanish.

Interestingly enough, the survey of the 30 maps and charts inside has nothing to do with US surveying efforts. Every single map was made by Spanish Jesuits of the Manila Observatory, a scientific research institute first set up in 1865 for weather forecast and earthquake research. Jesuits are known for their scholarly quest for knowledge while conducting missionary work, and this was no exception; the detail and accuracy of these maps are amazing, done under the supervision of Rev. Jose Algue, S.J., Director of the Manila Observatory.

Though 120 years to date, the string binding of the atlas is still intact and holding up the page ends well, unlike its paper which has turned yellowish and somewhat brittle. Turning the pages without care would result in tear and wear. In a format of 38cm long and 33cm wide, the atlas includes 30 maps, some of which have boxed-in sidebars detailing close-up sections. For example, there are nine sectional smaller charts that provide coastal depth sounding of the sea.

One of the maps, the first in the series, covers a large area of the Pacific Rim from eastern Siberia, Manchuria, Korea, Japan, coastal China, part of North America and much of the islands of the Pacific all the way to a large part of Australia. Five of the maps are of the entire Philippines, though each is for featuring different aspects of the country; for example ethnographic or orographic, a map depicting meteorological and seismographic stations, and one on mineral and agricultural resources. Many of the subsequent maps try to provide terrain of mountains, though not topographic, and river systems on the numerous islands. Notable on each map is the insignia or seal IHS, symbolizing Jesus Christ, which the Society of Jesus had long adopted as its fixed emblem. Encircling this symbol is added a compass design as background.

Map No.9 Manila Bay / 第九幅地圖：馬尼拉灣

Of particular interest to CERS and this author is the two-page map of Palawan, an island we are quite familiar with. On the northern top end there is no El Nido, let alone a resort of the same name. The closest marked town or settlement is Taytay. Puerto Princesa and its bay are separately enclosed as a chart with depth sounding of the entire bay. Honda Bay is called Bahia Honda and the tiny Shell Island which we visited a couple times is identified as Ia Shell. Cagayancillo, to which we sailed several times, some 200 km east of Palawan, is listed as Ia Cagayanes with some sandbars and reefs marked nearby. Even the narrow island gap for entry

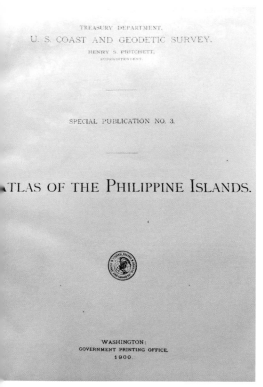

TREASURY DEPARTMENT,
U. S. COAST AND GEODETIC SURVEY.
HENRY S. PRITCHETT,
SUPERINTENDENT.

SPECIAL PUBLICATION NO. 3.

ATLAS OF THE PHILIPPINE ISLANDS.

WASHINGTON:
GOVERNMENT PRINTING OFFICE.
1900.

Inside title page / 封面內頁
Dividing the map of China in the past /
過去分割中國地圖

into a sheltered bay is correctly featured. At the bottom of Palawan, Balabac is included with all its nearby archipelagos.

Perhaps of significance missing on these maps are the Spratly Islands to the west of Palawan. It was made during a time when such atolls or reefs were of no consequence and with no squabbles or contention, let alone international tension. On the map, that entire ocean is marked Mar de la China, a hundred or so years before when it suddenly became known also as the Philippine Sea. But then a big island to the north is called Formosa rather than Taiwan. So, let us leave the arguments to the politicians, and their cohorts of followers. For us, we can admire the dedicated work of the Jesuit Fathers and those they trained, among whom I am one.

As a corollary from my learning with the Jesuits; if you sin, you can always redeem yourself by going to confession. So it is understandable that we see so many former aggressors take up moral high ground today.

(CERS has been using maps for decades on its exploration and has recently started collecting historical maps, not because they are old, but to help us interpret the history of the many places we now visit and conduct projects.)

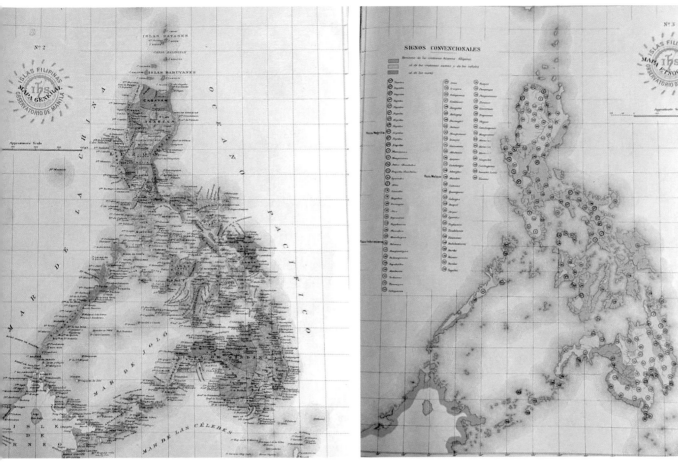

Map No. 2 General map of Philippines / 第二幅地圖：菲律賓概覽　　　　Map No.3 Ethnographic map / 第三幅地圖：民族人種地圖

菲律賓地圖集的推論

這標題已不言自明了。一九零零年由美國財政部的「美國海岸與地理測繪局」*(U.S. Coast and Geodetic Survey)* 發行，再由華盛頓的政府印刷辦公室出版的這本地圖集，封面那幾個浮凸燙金印刷字體的書名，卻以西班牙文標示：「菲律賓地圖集」*(ATLAS de FILIPINAS)*。

更有趣的是，書內三十幅地圖測繪與圖表，與美國在測繪上的努力，一點都扯不上關係。事實上，內文中的每一張地圖繪製，都出自「馬尼拉天文台」*(Manila Observatory)*——一個由西班牙耶穌會於一八六五年為氣象預報觀測與地震研究而創立的科學研究院。耶穌會在從事宣教工作之餘，向來在學術與知識領域的鑽研不餘遺力，而這份地圖集在「馬尼拉天文台」執行長荷西 . 阿爾格 *(José Algué)* 神父的指導下，無論精細與準確度，都一如以往般考究嚴謹，成效斐然，令人讚歎。

即便過了一百二十年，地圖冊的邊繩至今仍完好無損，沒有一頁脫落；只是紙張已不敵歲月磨損而泛黃，甚至有些脆化了，翻閱時得特別小心翼翼，否則容易撕毀而破損。地圖集的大小規格，長三十八公分、寬三十三公分，總計三十幅地圖，有些地圖的某個區域被局部放大，再另以邊欄格子來詳述相關細節與資訊，比方說，一張地圖上被分成九個區域性小圖解，說明沿岸的海洋深度。

地圖系列的第一張，涵蓋環太平洋的大片區域，從西伯利亞東邊、滿洲、朝鮮、日本、中國沿海、北美洲部分區域與太平洋周邊大部分海島，一直到澳洲的大面積土地。而單單整個菲律賓國土，便用了五幅地圖詳述，分別針對菲律賓的不同面向，譬如民族人種與地形特性、標示氣象學與測震學的研究站、敘述礦物與農業資源等。後續還有許多地圖提供山脈地貌，雖然不含地形特徵但不同島嶼上的水文河道，都詳列其中。其中值得關注的特色，是每一張地圖都附有一枚印上代表耶穌基督的「IHS」字母徽章，這是耶穌會沿用已久的標誌，徽章以羅盤設計為背景，把字母包圍起來。

對中國探險學會與本文作者而言，最感興趣的莫過於那兩頁篇幅的巴拉望 (Palawan) 地圖，那是我們所熟悉的大島。地圖的最北端並未標註愛妮島 (El Nido)，更別提與愛妮島同名的度假勝地了；地圖上標示出最接近當代的城鎮或村落是泰泰 (Taytay)。而公主港 (Puerto Princesa) 與其海灣，則被分別標註於附加圖表上，並詳列整個海灣的水深。宏達灣 (Honda Bay) 的舊名是「巴伊亞宏達」(Bahia Honda)，而我們去過好幾回的小小貝殼島，在地圖上則被標示為「貝殼」(Ia Shell)。我們也曾在卡加延西勞 (Cagayancillo)──位於巴拉望東方兩百公里之外的地點──揚帆渡海好幾回，在地圖上的名

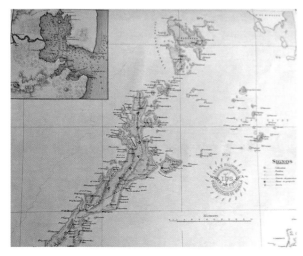

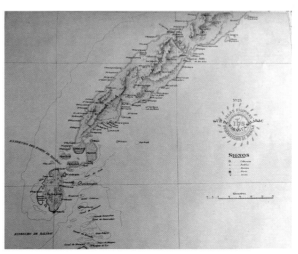

Map No.24 Northern Palawan / 第二十四幅地圖：北巴拉望　　　Map No.25 Southern Palawan / 第二十五幅地圖：南巴拉望

Map No. 24 PPS Bay detail /
第二十四幅地圖：公主港灣細部

稱卻是卡加延斯 (Ia Cagayanes)，而且還不忘註明周遭地形為沙洲與礁石。即便是取道狹長島嶼進入封閉海灣的海上峽谷，也被正確註記上。巴拉望底部的巴拉巴克 (Balabac) 與周邊群島，也都含括在內，無一缺漏。

唯獨巴拉望以西的南沙群島，在地圖上遍尋不著。事實上，製作這本地圖集時，這些環狀珊瑚島或礁石根本無足輕重，也引不起任何爭議或糾紛，更別提國際間的主權張力了。在地圖上，整片海洋的名稱是「南中國海」(Mar de la China)，但不知何故竟在一百多年後忽然被認定為菲律賓海。再往北一探，一個大島浮現於地圖上，島名「福爾摩沙」，而非台灣。我想，不如把一切爭論歸政治人物與他們的支持者吧；讓我們純然欣賞耶穌會的神父們所遺留的美好貢獻，與他們卓然有成的教育訓練；而我，何其有幸，曾是他們傳授的眾多學生之一。

以我對耶穌會的認知與信仰推論，你若犯罪，只要告解與懺悔，永遠可以罪得赦免，蒙受救贖。或許因為如此吧，難怪今天有那麼多「前侵略者」可以大言不慚，站在道德高地。

（中國探險學會數十年來在世界各地探索時，地圖不離手；我們近日開始蒐集歷史地圖，不是因為這些地圖陳舊古老，而是想藉此認清與詮釋許多當下尋訪與執行計劃之地的歷史背景。）

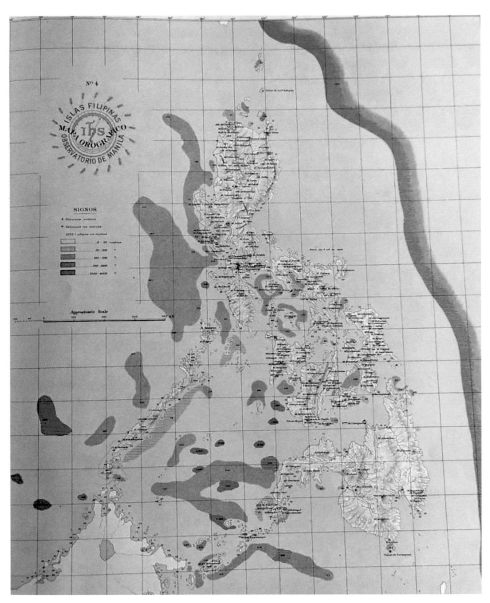

Map No.4 Orographic map / 第四幅地圖：地形特性地圖

犛
牛
年

YEAR OF THE YAK

Hong Kong, February 10, 2021

Hong Kong, February 10, 2021

YEAR OF THE YAK
With some reflections on trust

I was born in 1949 during the Year of the Ox. But having spent a good part of my life on the high plateau, I prefer to call it Year of the Yak. Better yet, that of the Wild Yak, which I have had the opportunity to observe numerous times in the wilds of Tibet. At times, it seems strange to me that we put so much emphasis on the year of birth, but not so much that of death. But then, people remember someone while living, not so much when they are gone.

As that matter goes, I would like to take this moment to reflect on several things, as the Chinese New Year is just around the corner, in two more days. First, contrary to popular belief, the Year of the Ox does not begin with the First Day of the New Year in the Chinese lunar calendar, commonly known as Chinese New Year. The Chinese zodiac is actually based on a solar calendar set up within a largely peasant population in the past for the benefit of the farmer who found the sun more relevant to the seasons of growing.

Each year is divided into 24 climate segments under the Chinese Almanac, and it begins with "Li Chun" or, as literally translated, "Standing Spring." Generally, this falls between February 3rd to

5th, but mainly on February 4 with some slight variations. For example, this year it begins around 11pm on February 3. But for convenience, these days most people, westerners included, consider the animal signs to start with the lunar New Year. (The mythical dragon is not quite an animal, but we will let it be the exception.)

By traditional and common belief, we are already in or stepping into, the Year of the Ox respectively. To return to the question of Year of Death that I raised above, I would comment on George Shultz, former Secretary of State of the U.S., who passed away at age 100 a few days ago, during the beginning of the Year of the Ox.

On December 11, two days before George Shultz turned 100, he wrote for the Washington Post ten points he had learned over the century of his life. They are all about trust, starting from childhood to old age, including stints in the marines during World War II, as a student at MIT before teaching there, as Dean of the University of Chicago Graduate School of Business, in business becoming President of Bechtel Corporation, then as Secretary of Labor, of Treasury, and finally of State. His career spanned fields from academia to business to government.

Shultz meeting Deng / 舒茲與鄧小平會面
Deng with Biden in background /
鄧小平會面，拜登於背景

Yak with calf / 犛牛與小牛

A few of his ten points stood out for me. One I relate here:

Trust is the coin of the realm. When trust was in the room, whatever room that was – the family room, the schoolroom, the locker room, the office room, the government room or the military room – good things happened. When trust was not in the room, good things did not happen. Everything else is detail.

One day, as secretary of state in the Reagan administration, I brought a draft foreign policy speech to the Oval Office for Reagan to review. He read the speech and said, "That's fine," but then began marking it up. In the margin on one page, he wrote "story". I asked what he meant. "That's the most important point," he said. Adding a relevant story will "engage your readers. That way, you'll appeal not only to their minds but to their emotions." Telling a story, he made me understand, helps make your case in a way no abstraction can: A story builds an emotional bond, and emotional bonds build trust.

Since a child, I wanted to be a storyteller, though knowing neither the reason nor the effect it could have. But now, I know.

If I were to look at the difficult times we now face, not only with the pandemic, but also the challenges facing China and the U.S., I recall it was under George Shultz's watch that great trust was built between the U.S. and China. America was able to set up listening posts in even distant Xinjiang's border with the then Soviet Union, in order to monitor nuclear tests and collect other sensitive intelligence. Today, Xinjiang instead has become a rhetorical battlefront, and trust is rare.

Joe Biden should perhaps put a small framed photo at his Oval office as reminder of the good old days. It was soon after China and the U.S. normalized their diplomatic relations on January 1 1979 that he first visited China as a junior Senator from Delaware as member of a Senate delegation. He also met for the first time with Deng Xiaoping. It was during Biden's conversation with the senior Chinese leader that Deng showed his willingness to permit the U.S.-equipped listening posts to monitor compliance with the SALT II arms limitation treaty.

That same year, as a young journalist living in the U.S. and on assignment for the Architectural Digest, I was able to visit and meet the first US Ambassador Leonard Woodcock at his relatively modest but beautiful Embassy Home in Beijing. Shortly thereafter, I participated in the 30th anniversary celebration of the People's Republic of China on October 1.

That was almost two years before I started exploring the Tibetan plateau and met my first yak in the spring of 1981. Now forty years later, no wonder I prefer calling this year the Year of the Yak. The yak is not only familiar to me, but has become something very close to my heart.

At this moment, I'm wearing a yak wool scarf with a photograph I took imprinted on it. The photo, taken in 1991, depicts a Tibetan in traditional costume milking a yak. Behind me hanging over my chair is a yak wool blanket. And in my refrigerator are a few wheels of yak cheese made by our Tibetan partner in Shangri-la, a project CERS

Wild Yak / 野犛

started almost twenty years ago. Over the years, we have also launched several expeditions to track down and study the little-known Wild Yak where they live, in the remotest and highest region of the plateau.

The Wild Yak, a globally threatened species still in great need of protection, may number as few as only 7,500 remaining. Much larger than its domestic cousin, game records cite Wild Yak bulls of over two meters at the shoulder in height. Nomads have claimed that they have seen some more than 2.5 meters tall at the shoulder. It is one of the least studied animals due to its remote and extreme habitat. However, Paul Buzzard and Bill Bleisch, under the auspices of CERS, have published several academic papers about this unique animal.

For some of us, the yak may be just a subject of study, a challenge to photograph, a fashion accessory, or something exotic for our taste buds. But for the Tibetans, it is an all-essential animal, ubiquitous on the high plateau. There are over 13 million domestic yaks in China, some 90% of the world's population.

It accounts for up to a quarter of the beef supply in the country and almost the same proportion of the country's milk production. Yak milk has up to 8% fat compared to regular milk at about 4%. Highly adapted to extreme

Baby yak learning to wean / 犛牛寶寶學習斷奶

Tibetan director at cheese site /
藏人總監在乳酪製作現場督導
Early batch yak cheese 2008 /
二零零八年的陳年犛牛乳酪

elevations up to 5,000 meters, a yak's lungs are about 1.4% of its total weight, as compared with 0.5% for a domestic ox.

The yak provides reliable and sure-footed transportation over difficult terrain and is the preferred riding animal for pregnant women who enjoy the relatively smooth and stable ride. Its hair, not only strong but water resistant as well, is used to make tents that can protect a family from the harshest of weather and climate.

Dairy products from yak milk are the basis for the nomad's diet. Cheese and curds – dried, soft, or smoked; milk – fresh, boiled or mixed with tea; and yoghurt, are delicacies reserved for special occasions or when special guests are visiting. They are to be found inside every nomad's black-hair tent. Yak butter is considered the most precious offering to the gods.

Yak meat, used in stews, made into sausage and, during the cold winter months, eaten raw, provides extra protein to an already high-protein diet. In an environment where the air is too rarefied for trees to grow, yak dung, when dried, is an extremely efficient fuel source, burning readily even in altitudes in excess of 5,000 meters above sea level.

Even after death, or after life I should say, the yak continues to provide its service. In many areas, individual vertebrae are used as tent pole supports and the horns of both the domestic and Wild Yak are used as milk containers. Four to six hides sewn together makes a coracle – a skin raft ideal for crossing the dangerous torrents on the plateau. While such crafts have now become obsolete, CERS in a last-ditch effort was able to rescue two specimens of these coracles after years of search. Now they preside at the entrance to the main hall of the CERS Center in Zhongdian, a.k.a. Shangri-la. Likewise, the yak tent which has become fewer and fewer has now taken a permanent display position inside our Center.

In short, for Tibetan nomads, the yak is by far their most important natural resource, an animal that they can trust to provide. It seems fitting here to end with the words of George Shultz, who died in this Year of the Yak. His last point, Number 10 in his essay, sums up trust.

"Trust is fundamental, reciprocal and, ideally, pervasive. If it is present, anything is possible. If it is absent, nothing is possible. The best leaders trust their followers with the truth, and you know what happens as a result? Their followers trust them back. With that bond, they can do big, hard things together, change the world for the better.

Musing on these words, I trust my colleagues, friends and supporters, and I hope they trust me. Together we can take CERS through good times and bad, through the Year of the Yak for now and then on into the future.

犛牛年 信任的省思

我出生於一九四九年，農曆牛年。但我的大半輩子每年都在高原度過，所以我想把自己的農曆生肖，稱之為犛牛年。「野犛」或許是更貼切的說法，因為我有太多機會在西藏的曠野荒漠見識過牠們。比起死亡之時，我們更重視出生之年，這一點至今仍令我倍感困惑。但話又說回來，我們常常念掛活著的人，對於亡者，記憶可能日漸沖淡。

時過境遷，眼看農曆新年再兩天就到了，我想藉此時機來檢視一些事。首先，與一般大眾深信不疑的觀點不同，牛年其實並非從農曆新年的首日開始算起。過去，在農民之間，中國黃道其實是依據陽曆來制定，因為他們發現農作物生長的季候，深受太陽的影響。

在中國年鑒下，一年分成二十四個節氣，從「立春」開始，望文生義，設「立」了「春」天。立春一般落在二月三日至五日，大部分時候是二月四日，但偶有差異與例外。比方說，今年立春首日，理當從二月三日的晚間十一點左右開始；但為了方便行事，現代大多數人，甚至包括西方人士也乾脆從農曆新年之始，開始推算起動物生肖。（當然，嚴格說來，神乎其神的龍其實不算動物，就讓它破例一次吧）。

不論從傳統或普遍觀念來看，我們都已經或正踏入牛年。回到我在引言提及的死亡之

年，我想從美國前國務卿喬治・舒茲 (George Shultz) 幾天前在牛年之始，以一百高齡辭世的事件，談談我的想法。

十二月十一日，在喬治・舒茲過一百歲生日前兩天，他為《華盛頓郵報》(The Washington Post) 寫了一篇文章，敘述他從過去一個世紀的人生中所領悟的學習，十大重點，娓娓道來，主旨都與「信任」相關。這些故事要從他的童年開始說起，一直到他年華老去；其中包括二戰期間他在海軍的日子、在麻省理工學院執教前的學生生涯、擔任芝加哥大學商學研究所所長、任職美國最大建築與工程公司貝泰 (Bechtel) 執行長、轉戰政壇後成為勞工部長、財務部長，最終成為美國國務卿；從軍旅至學術領域跨界至商場，再輾轉投身政壇，這一路走來的豐富閱歷。

十大重點的部分內容，於我心有戚戚。我把一些認同的段落，摘錄如下：

「信任是無價之寶。只要信任在，無論何處——家庭中、教室裡、更衣室、辦公室、政府部門或軍事單位——總會有好事臨到。可一旦信任缺席，準沒好事。信任是王道，其餘都是細節。」

「某日，身為雷根總統的國務卿，我帶了一份外交政策的演講初稿到總統辦公室讓雷根審閱。他讀了那份演講稿，點頭說好，隨

Woodcocks at home / 伍德科克家人攝於家中

Indoor yak tent in Zhongdian /
位於中甸中心的氂牛帳篷室內

少。但在中國探險學會的支持下，學會兩位研究員保羅‧巴澤 (Paul Buzzard) 與比爾‧布雷斯 (Bill Bleisch) 已前後發表過好幾篇與這隻獨特動物相關的學術專文。

對一些人而言，氂牛可能只是眾多研究主題之一，或一份攝影的挑戰，一件時尚的裝飾，或甚至一頓充滿異國風味、滿足味蕾的美食。但對西藏人而言，氂牛是高原上缺一不可、且無所不在的動物。在中國境內，有超過一千三百萬頭氂，占全球總氂牛數量的百分之九十有多。

在中國市場上，氂牛肉的供應量是牛肉的四分之一，但氂乳產量則與牛乳產量不相上下。與一般牛奶百分之四的脂肪含量相比，氂乳的脂肪含量高達百分之八。由於氂牛常年在五千公尺以上的極端高地生活，且適應良好，因此光是牠的肺重量，便占了總體重的百分之一點四，而一般家牛的肺，僅占體重的百分之零點五。

氂牛也是值得信賴與可靠的交通工具，特別在崎嶇難行的區域，更顯他「腳踏實地」的本性；牠是懷孕婦女的首選交通工具，一路走來，顛簸之途也走得四平八穩。氂牛的毛髮強韌又防水，是製作帳篷的主要材質，在嚴酷的極地天候下，守護帳篷裡的家庭。

氂牛奶所製成的乳製品，是西藏牧民基本的主食。其中包括乳酪

與乾凝乳——有鬆軟或煙熏口味；還有鮮奶，可以煮熱或配著茶一起喝；或優格等。這些可口的精緻美食，一般都保留到特殊場合或貴賓來訪時，才會端上桌，賓主一起享用。所以，在犛牛毛髮製成的黑色帳篷內，幾乎每一戶西藏牧民家庭裡，都可以找到這些乳製佳餚，其中，犛奶油甚至被視為祭拜神明的上等祭品，無比珍貴。

犛牛肉，一般以火燉煨，也用來醃製成香腸，有時候也在極端寒冷的月份直接生吃，在已經高蛋白的飲食中，再加碼提供額外蛋白質。在這樣一個空氣稀薄、樹木難以生長之地，乾燥的犛牛糞便，是最佳燃料源，即便在超越海拔五千公尺以上的高緯度地帶，沒有乾柴也能隨時烈火燃燒。

就算死了，也許我該說「來世」比較貼切，犛牛的服務與貢獻仍未停歇。在許多地方，犛牛的脊椎骨被用來當支撐帳篷的營柱，而無論家犛與野犛，牠們的角是盛裝牛奶的容器。除此以外，還有四到六片犛牛皮縫製而成的輕舟——這些皮革筏舟最適合跨越高原上危險的湍急河流，可惜這些小船已逐漸失傳而乏人使用——中國探險學會找了很久，費時耗力好幾年，最終搶救回兩艘犛牛皮製成

CERS artisan yak cheese cottage /
中國探險學會犛牛乳酪工匠小屋

Yak coracle next to Yangtze /
長江旁的犛牛皮筏輕舟

CERS coracle specimen /
中國探險學會收集的犛牛皮筏輕舟樣本

Yak raft on Lhasa River / 拉薩河上的犛牛皮筏舟

的輕舟。如今，兩片輕舟就在中國探險學會中甸（也被稱為香格里拉）中心的大廳入口處。犛牛帳篷也和這些皮筏輕舟的際遇相似，越來越稀有與罕見，現在也被置於我們中心，當成永久擺設。

簡而言之，對西藏遊牧族群而言，犛牛是他們最重要的天然資源，是他們全然信任、賴以為生的牲畜。走筆至此，讓這位亡於犛牛年的喬治・舒茲來總結這篇文章，或許是最貼切的安排。他行文至最後第十點，把「信任」歸根結底，做出結論：

「信任是一切根本與相互對等的關係，最好讓它無處不在。只要彼此信任，凡事都可能。但若失去信任，則萬事難成。最好的領袖會選擇信任他們的追隨者，你知道結果如何？他們的追隨者也對自己的領袖堅信不疑。在相互信任的關係下，他們可以一起做大事，共體時艱，為更好的未來而改變世界。」

我對這番話咀嚼再三，沉思久久。我信任我的同仁夥伴，我的朋友與支持者，我希望他們也信任我。我們要一起帶著中國探險學會同甘共苦，相互陪伴度過犛牛年，從現在一路走到未來。

Yak coracle in Lhasa River /
拉薩河上的犛牛皮筏輕舟
Tibetan girl in yak tent at Yangtze source 1985 /
於長江源頭犛牛帳篷內的西藏女孩，攝於一九八五年

華
光
廟

HUA GUANG TEMPLE

Tai O, Hong Kong – March 28, 2021

HUA GUANG TEMPLE
Discovering a little-known deity and his only temple in Hong Kong

Today is exactly one year since I took the last flight out of Yangon in Myanmar back to Hong Kong. Since then I have been home without traveling anywhere. Nonetheless, we managed to explore closer to home and started some small projects within our immediate community. And within that time, a few auspicious things happened that seemed to provide impetus for our new start-up projects. Karma you may call it.

It was Friday November 13, 2020, corresponding to the 28th day of the Ninth Moon in the lunar calendar. Be it a curse or a blessing, two things happened that affected five months of subsequent activities while I was holed up in Hong Kong during the pandemic. In fact, the effects may be quite long-term, at least for a year, and perhaps longer.

That morning, as usual I woke up early to watch the sunrise from my Hok Tsui (Cape D'Aguilar) studio. As winter was near, the sun had moved south and rose over the distant horizon with some glowing ray. Together with the distant lighthouse blinking off Waglan Isalnd, they seem to hint of bright times ahead. When the sun had reached about a fifteen degree altitude, I got up from a low cushioned chair, hoping to get myself another cup of latte. Just as I rose and turned, I felt something snap in my lower back. I had, once again, twisted my back!

I immediately knew that such impromptu disruption of an otherwise graceful pirouette would not only change my posture, but result in pain for days or weeks. When this happened, I could be bed-ridden for several days, barely able to carry my own weight without support of a walking cane.

The pain on this morning was deep, and I took notice, but stubborn as I always am, I continued with my routine and our scheduled departure for Lantau, the big island an hour's drive away from Hong Kong. We were to have a meeting over lunch with our new associates for culture conservation, Timmy and Chi Chuen, our collaborators. We had just procured the last wooden sampan of Hong Kong and had it delivered to them in the former fishing village of Tai O at the western end of Lantau. It seemed a perfect day for Xavier our filmmaker to add some footage of traditional rowing on this sampan.

Sunrise at Caper D'Aguilar / 鶴咀的日出

Lighthouse of Waglan Island / 橫瀾島的燈塔

Hok Tsui studio lookout / 鶴咀工作室的看台
Calendar on inside wall / 廟內牆上的掛曆

Pain in the back notwithstanding, I arrived in Tai O before noon. As lunch was set for 12:30, I took the opportunity, brought out my bicycle and cycled off. Just the week before, I had learned from a little-known book that a small temple on the remote edge of Tai O was the one and only temple in Hong Kong dedicated to the three-eyed fire god Hua Guang (Bright Light). This is the same deity revered by all people associated with performance of Cantonese operas, and I am an avid fan of such operas, having taken up small parts on stage as early as 1969 and 1972.

Off I went along the narrow path passing all the metal stilt houses of Tai O, cycling literally beyond the end of the village. It had been seven months since I had returned to Hong Kong, and to someone like me who had been on the road constantly for the previous fifty years, it had felt like a millennium. Though I could feel the pain in my lower back starting to burn, in less than ten minutes I arrived in front of the tiny temple Hua Guang.

I was shocked to see outside there were around thirty to forty people, seated on folding chairs or offering incense. There were even three roast pigs, partly divided up, on makeshift tables. And all around the temple were colorful flags on poles fluttering in the wind. Something was amiss. This was supposed to be a little-known temple.

"What's going on?" I quickly asked an older gentleman. "Today is the birthday of Hua Guang," came his answer. He introduced me to Mei, a middle-age lady who lived nearby and who was now in charge of maintaining the temple. Some ten years ago she saw the temple fall into total disrepair and took it upon herself to gradually revive it with few resources.

Mei led me into the small temple and pointed to a big Chinese calendar. "Today is the twenty-eighth day of the ninth moon, so it is Hua Guang's birthday," said Mei. Mei went on to tell me that even when asked by passers-by about the temple and Hua Guang deity, she would draw a blank. She had long hoped that someone would enlighten her with the stories of Hua Guang, so that she could explain the temple more accurately to others. I told her right away that we would try.

I was taken aback by such an auspicious and impromptu coincidence. How could I have just injured my back, insisted on making my appointment, rushed out before lunch to have a brief look at an unknown temple, and caught it just on the one day of celebration in a year. I rushed right back to my friends and filmmaker. "Xavier, there's no more lunch, let's go!" I hurried him along. Before long, we were back at the temple site just as everyone was packing up to leave.

National & Hua Guang flags / 國旗與華光誕旗海
Wide flags honor Hua Guang / 旗海慶賀華光誕

I knew at that time that I must come back again, and again and again, not only to make a record of this somewhat dilapidated yet special temple, but to help restore it and make it better known to Hong Kong and beyond. And I quietly promised myself that the 28th of the 9th Moon in 2021 during the next birthday celebration of Hua Guang would become a special event and that many of the people who revered the deity would be represented.

While my body and back pain intensified later that day and evening, my heart was filled with joy that CERS had discovered yet another worthy project despite the pandemic and stay-at-home order in Hong Kong. In less than two weeks, I was finally back to normal, out of bed, walking straight. I started my new odyssey by returning to the temple to offer my joss stick in thanks to Hua Guang for offering me the chance to make a contribution to an otherwise little-known temple with great stories.

Over the next three months, I was able to find out more about the history of Hua Guang, an important deity for centuries yet little-known even to those who observe and revere him today. We have coordinated not only the upgrade of the temple's small halls, but also printed an informative leaflet for everyone to better understand the history of Hua Guang. Below are some of the more unique stories that we were able to gather and share with everyone.

The Hua Guang (Wah Kwong in Cantonese) Temple in Tai O, Lantau Island is the only historical temple in Hong Kong dedicated to honoring the Daoist and Buddhist deity Hua Guang. A tablet dating back to 1896 of the Qing Dynasty remains inside the temple and gives evidence of its long history.

Hua Guang originally was a wick in an oil lamp in front of the Bodhisattva. Listening to Buddhist scriptures being chanted day after day, Hua Guang transformed into an elf of fire and reincarnated four times. Later, Bodhisattva cast a spell on Hua Guang who gained a human body and extraordinary fighting skills. Finally, he became the Fire Marshal under the Jade Emperor in heaven. In Daoism, he is also a martial general. Hua Guang is revered by many in coastal China, including in Guangdong, Guangxi, Fujian, Hainan, Hong Kong and Macau. Some people even name their children with the character "Hua" as if the child is being adopted by Hua Guang in order to acquire his protection.

Many professions, in particular Cantonese opera actors, orchestra musicians, stage craftsmen and artisans, especially those in need of avoiding of fire, like those working with paper crafting, ceramics and pottery, scaffolding workers, as well as select martial artists and lion dancers, and even fishermen in Hainan - they all hold the three-eyed Fire God Hua Guang in revere. In the past, apart from celebrating the Birthday of Hua Guang, people would perform Hua Guang Jiu once every decade, to pray for Hua Guang's protection from the harm of fire.

According to legends from as early as the late Yuan and early Ming Dynasties (13th to 14th centuries), the deity Hua Guang (Wah Kwong in Cantonese) has been revered and his stories have been widely circulated by Chinese. During the Yuan Dynasty, Yang Jingxian created a drama entitled "Xi You Ji" (Pilgrimage to the West), which depicted a scene of Hua Guang disrupting the Heavenly Palace. Some scholars suggest that Wu Chengen might have been inspired by Yang Jingxian's earlier depiction of Hua Guang after comparing Yang's drama and Wu's novel of "Xi You Ji". From disruption of the Heavenly Palace, use of Taishang Laojun's stove for magical eyes and

Hua Guang temple altar / 華光廟祭壇

eventual elevation to being an official, these experiences of Hua Guang are all replicated in the Monkey King's story.

The Ming Dynasty novel "Nan You Ji" (Pilgrimage to the South) provides further details and descriptions regarding the birth, endeavors and legacy of Hua Guang. A deity born with exceptional magical talents and fighting skills, such as Fire Magic and an eye that could see all three worlds, Hua Guang subdued many evil spirits on earth as well as in heaven. With trials and tribulations, like the rescue of his mother, he was ultimately given a seat of honor as the Fire God by the side of the Emperor in heaven.

The most widely circulated legend among Cantonese opera circles also provides the following romantic story:
As a Cantonese opera was being performed, the very loud sound of the drums and gongs and singing reached heaven and disturbed the peace of the Heavenly Emperor. He thus ordered Hua Guang, the Fire God, to descend to earth and burn down the theater.

Hua Guang arrived at the scaffolding of the theater, but instead of carrying out his mission, he was captivated by the drama and songs of the opera. He hesitated in executing the order from the Emperor and decided to spare the troupe. Instead, he taught them to burn incense and paper offerings to heaven. He also instructed them to wear red pants, so as to pretend to be burning. (This is the origin of the phrase "wearing red pants," meaning "starting from the bottom"). The Emperor, seeing smoke ascending to heaven, thought the mission was accomplished. As a result, Cantonese Opera was saved and has survived to this day.

From then on, it has been standard practice for the statue of Hua Guang to preside backstage among Cantonese Opera troupes for protection and prayers. And the 28th Day of the 9th Moon is revered as the Birthday of Hua Guang, on which day it is customary that a special production of "Birthday Feast on the Mountain of Fragrant Flowers" would be performed to celebrate the event, requiring participation of far more artists than a usual performance.

Hong Kong has hundreds of temples and shrines throughout its villages and towns, but only one authentic Hua Guang Temple. To preserve its history and legacy is important not only for the professions affiliated to his worship, but also as a unique demonstration of our region's diverse history, heritage and identity.

Spirituality provides one of the most important human sustenance beyond our current façade of infrastructure and material wealth. Faraway and distant as Hua Guang Temple is, it should hold a special place for those who make the effort to visit it and for all, not so much as another tourist site, but as a place of history and of worship. Hua Guang literally means "bright light", perhaps the morning lights I saw from my studio was indeed a light from Hua Guang.

華光廟

發現香港鮮為人知的神祇與其唯一廟宇

去年此時，我從緬甸搭乘最後一班從仰光離境的飛機，返回香港，今天剛好滿一年。自此我便待在家裡，哪兒也沒去。但也並非足不出戶，我們仍努力安排一些勘察小計劃，就在離家不遠的鄰里社區。說來巧合，這段時間剛好接連發生一些喜出望外的好事，冥冥中似乎為我們剛起步的計劃注入契機與動力。或許你可以稱之為善緣吧！

我記得很清楚，那天是二零二零年十一月十三日，禮拜五；農曆九月二十八。我當時正因為全球疫情而不得不自我囚禁在家，當天發生了兩件事，分不清是詛咒或祝福，卻足足影響了我後續五個月的活動與行程。事實上，影響力恐怕比預期更長遠，少說一年，或許還更久。

我一如往常般晨起，在鶴咀的工作室等看東升的旭日。冬天的腳步近了，太陽開始偏南移，遠方天際有些光芒，緩然升起，我遠眺橫瀾島，島上燈塔照射的亮光，與日光相互輝映，彷彿預示了未來前程將一片光明燦爛。太陽升至十五高度角時，我從低矮的椅子上起身，想給自己倒第二杯拿鐵咖啡。站穩後一轉身，突感下背部一陣異狀。我想我該是再度閃到腰了。

我當下立刻明白，這華麗轉身在毫無準備下出現的閃失，不只改變了我的姿勢，還會

讓我痛不欲生好幾天或甚至好幾週。每每發生這種狀況，我都得臥床數日，生活起居都得仰賴拐杖的支撐，否則寸步難行。

我注意到今早的疼痛來得猛又烈，但固執如我，仍堅持完成既定行程，按照我們事先的規劃，從香港島驅車一小時，前往大嶼山。我們當天還安排了午餐會議，要與新進會員與我們的合作對象添明、志泉，一起討論文物保存等問題。因為我們不久前才剛成功取得香港最後一艘木舢舨，舢舨已於日前送到大嶼山西部、前身為漁村的大澳。一切似乎都到位了，影片製作人李伯達 (Xavier) 還可補上一些「在傳統舢舨上搖櫓」的畫面片段，簡直是個良辰吉日。

雖然背痛持續，我仍依約在中午前抵達大澳。午餐將於十二點半開始，我把握時機牽出腳踏車，開始騎著四處晃蕩。才一個禮拜前，我無意間讀到一本名不見經傳的書，提及大澳某處偏僻角落，有家全香港唯一主祀三眼火神華光大帝的古廟。華光大帝其實就是粵劇戲迷尊崇有加的祖師爺，而我正好是粵劇的超級粉絲，還曾在一九六九年至一九七二年間粉墨登場，客串幾個小角色。

騎進狹窄小巷，越過大澳村一間間鐵皮高腳屋，一路騎到村尾盡頭。我掐指一算，待在香港已七個月，想我這麼一個前半生五十年歲月都在旅途中行進的人，這段悶在家的時間何止度日如年，簡直像千年那麼久。即便下背部仍隱隱作痛，而且開始感覺劇痛了，但我仍在十分鐘內抵達華光小廟前。

只見廟口前竟擠滿了人，大約三、四十個信眾排排坐在折疊椅上，也有人驅前上香，如此熱鬧場景，倒是令我訝然吃驚。門前三隻燒豬，稍微斬件擺在臨時湊合的桌上。古廟四周插滿彩色旗幟，迎風招展。我暗自思忖，這應該只是一間少人聞問的小廟，如此排場與鼎盛之香火，似乎有些不尋常，我總覺事有蹊蹺。

「發生什麼事了？」我向一名老者探詢。「今天是華光大帝誕辰日，」他回答，接著引薦梅姐讓我認識。梅姐是住附近的一名中年女性，負責打理這家廟宇。大約十年前，她眼看這家小廟年久失修，於是自動自發，以不多的資源，一點一滴、慢慢修復，還其風貌。

梅姐領我走進小廟，指著一個大大的農曆表，說：「今天是農曆九月二十八，是華光大帝的誕辰日。」梅姐坦誠相告，常常有路過民眾問起這座廟宇歷史與華光大帝，她因一無所知，也只能無言以對。她祈盼多年，希望有人可以把華光大帝的故事背景告訴她，好讓她將來面對外人的好奇探詢時，知道如何把華光廟解說得更準確。我當下對梅姐允諾，將盡力協助。

頃刻間，我對這些因緣具足的天時地利，與臨時起意的一連串巧合，驚詫得難以置信。背部受傷，堅持赴約，午餐前衝出門，騎到名不見經傳的小廟看一看，居然躬逢其盛趕上了一年一度的慶典。我不假思索衝回朋友店中，拉著朋友和影片製作人，十萬火急：「伯達，沒有午餐了，馬上跟我走！」我們一行人趕回華光廟時，信眾們已動身準備離開。

我知道我還必須再來好幾次，一次又一次重訪，不僅是為了記錄這間破舊又獨特的小廟，也為要協助修復它，讓更多香港人與外人更認識華光廟。我默默自我期許，明年此時，二零二一年農曆九月二八的華光大帝誕辰日，要讓這一天成為一場特殊活動，召聚更多尊崇華光大帝的人，一同共襄盛舉。

那一天稍後直到晚上，我的背痛加劇，身體也疲累，但一想到中國探險學會竟在疫情肆虐香港與居家不外出的禁令當前，還能發掘如此值得探究的計劃，我內心喜不自勝。不到兩週，我的背痛終於復原，可以如常下床，好好走路。於是，我又蠢蠢欲動，展開全新而漫長的漂泊之旅，回到華光廟，點上一炷香，感謝華光大帝賜我良機，讓我為一間寂寂無聞但深藏不露的小廟，做一些貢獻。

接下來的三個月內，我發掘出更多有關華光大帝的歷史，原來許多祭拜祂、崇敬祂的信眾粉絲，對這位流傳好幾世紀的重要神明，所知不多。我們不僅合力修建寺廟小殿堂，還印製了介紹華光廟的傳單，讓大家對華光大帝的歷史有更深入的了解。以下是我們搜集來想與大家分享的故事——精彩而獨特。

華光廟位於大嶼山的大澳村，是香港唯一敬奉道教與佛教神祇華光大帝的歷史古廟。廟內存放一片板子，上面標註的日期可追溯至一八九六年的清朝時期，由此可見其久遠身世。

華光本是菩薩前一盞油燈的燈芯。因終日反復聆聽佛教徒日復一日的誦經，華光轉化而成火神，並歷經四次轉世而為人，爾後接受菩薩施法，並被賦予異於常人的武功。最終，他在玉皇大帝的天宮裡成了火神統帥，護法天界；華光在道教傳統裡也被視為一

Cantonese opera actors with Mei ／ 梅姐與粵劇名伶
Celebrating Hau Guang birthday / 慶祝華光誕

Tablet from 1896 inside temple /
一八九六年建成的廟內牌匾

名武將。中國沿海包括廣東、廣西、福建、香港與澳門，至今仍可找到許多敬奉華光的信眾。有些人甚至刻意以「華」字來為孩子命名，彷彿藉此便可被華光大帝收養，以獲神明庇護。

眾多職業類別中，尤以粵劇演員、弦樂樂師、舞台技師與工匠，特別那些需要遠避火源的工作，譬如紙料工藝、瓷器與陶器、舞台搭棚工人、精選的武術指導與舞獅舞者，甚至包括海南島的漁夫——他們都供奉三眼火神華光大帝。過去，除了慶祝華光大帝誕辰以外，信眾還會每隔十年便舉辦「華光醮」神戲，向這位火神大帝祈福求庇護，免受火患災害。

根據元末明初（十三至十四世紀期間）的傳說，信奉神祇華光的人很多，而祂的各種事跡也在中國民間傳誦不絕。元朝作家楊景賢曾撰寫《西遊記》雜劇，其中一幕便是敘述華光如何大鬧天宮。有些學者在比較了楊景賢的《西遊記》雜劇與後來由吳承恩撰寫的文學巨著《西遊記》，主張吳承恩想必受楊景賢早期對華光大帝的描繪所啟迪。從大鬧天宮，再以太上老君的煉丹爐換得火眼金睛，到最後謀得官品，被封為齊天大聖，這些原是華光大帝的歷程都被吳承恩複製成齊天大聖孫悟空的故事裡。

明朝小說《南遊記》則提供更多與華光大帝相關的細節與敘述，包括祂的出生、豐功偉業與貢獻。神明一出生便擎天架海，本領

Performance for Hua Guang / 華光誕演出

非凡又武功高強，譬如祂的火魔法，與同時看穿三個世界的眼睛，無論人間或天府，華光大帝收服眾多妖魔鬼怪，法力無邊。華光大帝勇於面對各種危難艱險，譬如拯救母親的孝行事跡，最終為祂贏得天府的一席之地，在玉皇大帝身邊當火神。

其中一則是在粵劇行流傳千古的浪漫故事。話說大戲開演時，敲鑼打鼓與歌聲幾達穿雲裂石時，強大音量響徹「天際」而驚擾了玉皇大帝。玉皇大帝不悅，於是差派火神華光，下落凡間去把劇院燒了。

華光抵達劇院的搭檯前，原該奉命「火」速執行任務，但祂竟深受大戲的鑼鼓喧天與歌聲所吸引。華光猶豫了，對玉皇大帝的聖旨產生動搖，而決定放過劇院，不燒了。華光想出了替代方案，祂教導這群人如何燒香、燒金紙，獻祭予天府。祂還指示他們穿紅褲子，假意被火燒，喬裝掩飾。自此這說法便成了「紅褲子出身」之起源，意味著「從基層做起」。玉皇大帝瞥見焚紙燒香的裊裊升煙上達天庭，誤以為華光的使命已達成。因此，粵劇逃過一劫，留存至今。

從此以後，粵劇後台總能找到華光大帝的神像——虔敬供奉與祭拜，祈福保平安——已是戲班普遍的信仰。每逢農曆九月二十八，眾人奉為華光誕辰日，按習俗演出《香花山大賀壽》，這項慶華光誕的特別節目，動用的演員遠比一般劇目為多。

香港鄉鎮與都市的廟宇與聖祠，不下數百間，但正宗的華光廟，僅此一家。保存這份宗教歷史與資產很重要，不只是為了粵劇專業領域所追求的信仰，也展示我們區域性獨樹一幟的多元歷史、文化遺產與身份認同。

靈性提供我們深刻悠遠的人文滋養，超越任何有形有體、物質財富的存在與表象。無論華光廟位處多麼遙遠與偏僻，對每一位不辭顛簸而前來訪視這間廟宇的人，這確實是個值得親臨的特殊之處，它不太像旅客蜂擁而至的景點，卻是個瞻望歷史與崇拜之地。華光的字面意義已昭然明示，乃「明光照耀」之意……誰曉得呢，或許我從工作室望出去的那道絢麗晨光，竟真是華光之光！

Statue of Hua Guang / 華光大帝像　　　　　　Alter honoring Hua Guang / 華光廟內香火

重新發現與探索巴拉望

RE-DISCOVERY AND EXPLORATION OF PALAWAN

Hong Kong – March 2021

RE-DISCOVERY AND EXPLORATION OF PALAWAN

It was exactly five hundred years ago in 1521, also on this month of March, that Ferdinand Magellan, the Portuguese explorer, first "discovered" the Philippines and put it onto a western map. By then three ships was all that remained of his fleet of five ships, after losing one ship in a storm and another to desertion, having spent over a year at sea and circumnavigated three-quarters of the world.

Within weeks, he had been able to carry out a missionary crusade and convert a tribal chief and his Cebuano tribe. While near Cebu trying to fight another tribal chief Lapulapu, the Mactan island native and traditional enemy of his newly converted flock, Magellan was hit by a poison arrow. (Some accounts have it that he was killed by an enemy spear.) He died on April 27.

Arrow or spear, now without the famous historical maritime expedition leader, the endeavor continued to explore the Philippines. Seven weeks later, the remaining team sailed south and landed in Palawan. Upon leaving Palawan, two ships would continue westward, and eventually one ship, the Victoria, returned to Europe, captained by one of Magellan's subordinate officers, Juan Sebastian Elcano, a Basque native of Seville, completing what is considered to be the first circumnavigation of the world.

Our landing in Palawan was far less significant and with little ceremony, let alone missionary quests. We were unarmed, unlike the Spanish pioneers five centuries before, and I was converted by the natives - my domestic helper Jocelyn, who sometimes went home to Palawan on her vacation. She brought back images of the islands near her home, with pristine turquoise water, transparent below and exposing some beautiful coral beneath.

Those images caught my fascination and soon I launched our first fact-finding trip to Palawan. That was in September 2014, some six years ago. While staying at Jocelyn's rather spartan abode, barely hooked up with electricity and with no running water, I began to explore the coastal region of the island, roughly half the size of Belgium, and almost exactly the same size as the state of Connecticut.

Within a few short months, I returned with a much larger team, ten members in total, to conduct a shake-down cruise of the HM Explorer II, an outrigger boat we commissioned, built in record time of less than eight months.

Early load to Palawan / 晨早貨運至巴拉望　　　HM Explorer II with inflatables / 「HM 探險家 II 號」與充氣船

This boat, over the next several years, would serve as our home away from home, island hopping around the coastline of Palawan, as well as sailing some two hundred kilometers east to the distant islands around Cagayancillo. We also went to the extreme north to the limestone paradise of El Nido, and to the deep South, a predominantly Muslim community, as we explored islands off the southern tip of Palawan near Balabac.

Meanwhile our caving team from Yunnan came to assist a local community to map two caves and conduct resource inventory and analysis, which subsequently led to the opening of these caves for both local and foreign visitors. For the better part of two years, our staff anthropologist would lead us into the jungle hamlets of the indigenous Batak people, barely 300 individuals remaining. We would attend a number of their secret ceremonies as well as recording remnants of their fast-disappearing culture, including bark cloth making and wild bee honey collecting. We have even experimented several bamboo rafting trips operated by the Batak. CERS has made several films on the Batak to date and we feel fortunate that the Batak has become our culture conservation focus in Palawan.

Coral near shore / 近岸珊瑚
Coral fish / 珊瑚魚
Clear pristine water / 水色清澈

Maoyon, the largest river in Palawan has become our home as we anticipated many years and decades of involvement on the island. Our CERS base stands on ten hectares of riverside land two bends in the river away from the blue ocean, it offers shelter and harbor for our boats in case a typhoon should hit, which is more than a yearly event in the Philippines. There are over a thousand coconut palms on our land, and natural old-growth mangrove forest grows at our margin to four or five stories tall. Fireflies and tropical birds are around year-round, and likewise the huge Palawan Flying Fox bats that glide by after dark. The biggest surprise was when we hired someone to sink a well within our premises; we hit a natural treasure of fresh water, continuously gushing up to the surface like a pristine spring since 2016.

Our land, accessible only by our own shuttle boats, is now built up with two large villas, three floating lodges, two treehouses, as well as an area dedicated as our Batak cultural village, replicating the Batak style of thatch-roofed house while surrounded by fish ponds with waterlilies. The village is intended to be operated and run in the future by the Batak people themselves. Several groups have so far visited our site and projects in the area, including a university vice president, deans and professors. The future of Palawan as one of CERS's experiential learning centers for students is not far away, that is, once the pandemic is under control.

Indeed, some five years of work since I first saw Palawan may seem a long time. But looking back, what is five years for someone who is now into his seventh decade? Let alone when I look back on Magellan, who first landed in the Philippines in 1521. Considering that, five years is nothing at all. Perhaps in another 500 years, someone will look at our small contribution to this wonderful land and feel the same way that I do today reminiscing about the famous maritime explorer.

重新發現與探索巴拉望

一五二一年，距離今天恰好五百年前，連月份也適逢三月，葡萄牙探險家麥哲倫 (Ferdinand Magellan) 首度「發現」菲律賓，並將此新發現標示於西方地圖上。原來啟程出航的五艘探險船艦，歷經超過一年在海上環繞了四分之三個世界，截至當時，僅剩三艘，其中一艘被暴風雨吞噬，另一艘則因艱苦和意見不合而離去。

抵達當地後，才短短幾週，麥哲倫的宣教運動湊效，菲律賓的宿霧族酋長與其部落紛紛皈依有成。麥哲倫在宿霧附近，遇上另一酋長拉普拉普 (Lapulapu) 以及麥克坦 (Mactan) 島原著民，他們原是不久前皈依天主的宿霧信眾的世代宿敵，雙方發生激戰，麥哲倫亂中被毒箭射擊而喪命，也有些史料記錄麥哲倫是被敵方長矛攻擊致死；死於四月二十七日。

毒箭也好，長矛也好，反正探險隊已痛失了一位名垂千史、海洋長征的探險領袖，但對菲律賓的探險事業沒有因此中斷，仍舊持續奮進。七週以後，麥哲倫的團隊往南航行，停靠巴拉望。離開巴拉望時，兩艘探險艦隊往西前進，最終，只剩下由麥哲倫屬下一位軍官胡安・埃爾卡諾 (Juan Sebastian Elcano) 掌舵的「維多利亞號」，平安返回歐洲；這位塞維亞 (Seville) 土生土長的巴斯克 (Basque) 人，繼承首領遺志，完成環繞地球的首次壯舉。

相對之下，我們登陸巴拉望的行動，顯然平平無奇，沒有儀式感，更別提宣教使命了。我們身上沒有任何武器，不像五世紀前的西班牙拓荒者那般來勢洶洶；我沒有讓誰皈依，自己反倒被一名當地人說服而「皈依」了——我的幫傭喬思林。喬思林來自巴拉望，偶爾返鄉休假後歸來，她會把住家鄰近島嶼的照片帶回來讓我看，水面波光瀲灩，澄澈見底，美麗的珊瑚隱然可見。

這些照片看得我心神蕩漾，不久後我便著手規劃前往巴拉望的「實況調查」之首航。那大概是二零一四年九月，距今大約六年多。我住在喬思林略顯簡陋的房子裡，供電不足且沒有自來水。巴拉望島嶼面積大約是比利時的一半，幾乎與美國康乃狄克州 (Connecticut) 大小一致。我開始沿著島嶼海岸探索去。

短短幾個月後，第二次旅程時，我的團隊已壯大為十個成員，準備著手為我們的「HM 探險家 II 號」船進行試航計劃，這是一艘只用了八個月內便完成製造的舷外浮體船。往後好幾年，在巴拉望沿岸跳島遊覽時，這隻小艇成了我們家以外的家。它更承載我們一行人航行向東兩百公里外、靠近卡加延島 (Cagayancillo) 的各

Early cave exploration / 早期的洞穴探索
Bamboo rafting with Batak / 與巴達克族人划竹筏
Palawan Villa / 巴拉望別墅

個離島。我們也曾遠赴最北端、愛妮島 (El Nido) 的石灰岩天堂，再往巴拉望最南端、靠近巴拉巴克 (Balabac) 周遭以穆斯林社群為主的島嶼。

與此同時，遠從雲南過來的學會洞穴探險團隊過來協助一個當地社群為兩處洞穴測量和製作地圖，並進行洞穴資源調查與分析，評估後著手為當地居民與國外遊客開發這些洞穴。近兩年的大部分時間，我們團隊的人類學家帶領我們深入巴達克 (Batak) 原始部落的森林村落裡；所有部落村民僅存大約三百名。我們參與了好幾場屬於他們族人的神秘儀式，同時記錄下他們急速流失的傳統文化，其中包括樹皮衣製作與野蜜採集。我們也嘗試了幾趟由巴達克族人操作主導的竹筏泛舟行程。其實，中國探險學會迄今為止為巴達克族人製作了不少影片，我們很榮幸能有巴達克族成為我們在巴拉望的文化保育中心員工。

茂雲河 (Maoyon) 是巴拉望最長的河流，這數十年來在巴拉望啟動各種島嶼規劃與工作時，這條河已然成為我們的家。中國探險學會在巴拉望設了個基地，就在茂雲河畔十公頃的土地上，再往下兩處河灣，大河便匯入蔚藍的海洋；考量菲律賓每年颱風頻繁，風強雨大時，這個基地成了船隻最佳避風港。放眼望去，我們這塊土地上長滿了椰子樹，至少上千棵，而周遭的邊緣地帶，則是已然遠古的天然紅樹林，看來有四、五層樓的高度。螢火蟲與各

種熱帶鳥類一年四季都在，還有巴拉望狐蝠的巨型蝙蝠，也常年在黑夜中出沒。除了這些嬌客帶來的驚喜，還有一件最令我們驚詫的事——某日請人來挖井，竟無意間挖出一處天然噴泉，汨汨流水從二零一六年「源遠流長」至今，宛若沁人泉水。

想要抵達我們這塊土地，得仰賴我們的接駁船隻才到得了；如今，我們還蓋起了兩棟別墅，三間水上小屋，兩間樹屋，以及一座專屬的巴達克族文化村，複製巴達克族的茅草屋頂，圍繞四周的是佈滿睡蓮的魚塘。我們希望將來讓巴達克族人自行經營與管理這村落。這段期間的運作，已吸引好幾個團隊來此觀察與了解我們在這區域的工作，其中包括一間大學的副校長、主任與教授們。中國探險學會已將巴拉望的未來，列為實驗性教學中心，只要疫情控制得當，這項目標便有望落實，指日可待。

從我第一次踏上巴拉望至今，匆匆已過五個年頭。如今回首，五年，之於一名年過七旬者如我，算得了什麼？更別提回到更久遠的過去看看麥哲倫了，他第一次抵達菲律賓時是一五二一年呢！這麼一想，五年實在不足掛齒。或許再過五百年後吧，但願人們發現我們為這塊美麗的土地所付出的微薄貢獻時，也和我今天緬懷起曾經名聞一時的航海探索者一般，感同身受。

Batak lodge with ponds / 設有池堂的巴達克小屋

一九八四年，從海南出海

OUT TO SEA FROM HAINAN circa 1984

Hong Kong – March 31, 2021

OUT TO SEA FROM HAINAN circa 1984

It seems amazing that today we write, read or talk about distant places without personally having been there. I have been to China since 1974 countless times, including into some of the least known remote places, yet refrain from writing or speaking about such places with authority, knowing well that things are dynamic and change all the time. My knowledge, even gained first hand, has limitation in time and scope, let alone coming with biases of perspective and incomplete knowledge. So we must leave the defining remarks to those who see themselves as the brightest, who know it all, and believe they have a neutral agenda and stand on the highest moral ground.

It was January 1984 when I launched an expedition to Hainan Island, covering briefly all sixteen counties and two cities. However, the most important aspect of that trip was to penetrate into some of the more remote villages of the Li minority, at that time numbering around one million. I had already finished two major expeditions at the National Geographic, in 1982 and 1983, and this new work was again under the auspices of the National Geographic Magazine.

The work with the Li people was rather expansive and extensive, including four hours of film footage that I shot on the side, besides fulfilling my writing and photography assignment. Though the

Wooden boat being buiit / 正在興建的木船

footage was shot on mini-VHS tapes and so was of marginal quality, it was recently made into 16 short episodes as a record of the past. Together with subsequent work on as many as a dozen additional trips to Hainan from 2007 to present, they would be organized as an archive at our Hainan Hongshui Li Village where CERS has restored an ensemble of 18 traditional thatch-roofed houses.

However, among my notes there are still plenty of worthy "vignettes" - select sections from which a brief narrative can become an excellent record for comparisons by future scholars and scientists. One such section is the record of an overnight trip I took out to sea with two fishing trawlers. Obviously the account is anecdotal; I could only be on one ship, thus my account was based on observations and interviews with the captain and crew of that one ship. Nonetheless, it stands as an important record of the past.

Most of my expeditions, both during my National Geographic years or thereafter with CERS, lasted weeks or months. The notes below are taken from two days. It is perhaps one of the highlights worth remembering during my Hainan expedition of 1984, noted here in almost complete form, word for word.

NOTES TAKEN BETWEEN JAN 11-12, 1984 AT YU CUN VILLAGE NEAR SANYA AND AT SEA

At nearby market, Cuttlefish Y1.30 per catty, Large paired prawn（對 蝦）Y4.00 per catty with each catty around eight to ten pieces, Jellyfish Y0.70 per catty. Betel nuts Y5.00 for 100 pieces.

Yu Village chief Ye Zhenxin (47) home is two story building, built for three years. Nearby many houses unfinished and vacant. He said as policy allowed new homes to be constructed, everyone started building. Then sudden word came, new policy announced that fishermen can now own their boat, so everyone quickly stopped construction and redirected their money to building boats in order to make more money. Ye is so-called "Deng" people and speaks Cantonese, and has lived here for generations. Cannot tell where in China they originated from. Eight in his household with five children and one grandchild. Two kids are fishermen on boats, one teaching at a high school, one still studying at school. Ye's account:

Trawlers usually work in pairs. Each boat has a crew of at least 12-15. As it was not privately owned in the past and under a commune system, crews tended to be larger then. Now, because of benefits directed toward individuals sharing profits, each boat has fewer hands while efficiency is improved and likewise financial return. Boat needed to use lights and boats circle fishing requires more people, usually 18. Small boats for circling with 20-40HP engines. Locally, no one uses boats with sail anymore. Those seen are all from outside. Boats are made mainly locally, but with some made at Yang Jiang along coast of Guangdong. Some boats with sail came from outside are used as cargo ships, with sails made in Haikou.

Today, almost 100% of the boats are privately owned. But up until early 1983, they still belonged to the local brigade. By 1984, prices began to fall for these boats, so families with large number of members would purchase the boat. Smaller families would team together and buy one. Each boat is around 7-8 tons, but some are over 10 tons. Beginning in 1982, the brigade built on its own a lot of smaller boats due to policy being delegated to more local regions. These are from 12-20 Horse Power boats. A 12HP boat would cost around seven thousand Yuan. It must be paid up at once, so if you have not enough money then can get a loan from the bank. Most families live on the boat. But beginning in 1980, each household got an allocation with housing. Some large families are lucky to have more than one house.

During Chinese New Year and special holidays, all boats return to port. Typhoon season from August to October.

Trawlers working jointly / 拖網漁船聯手行動

Sorting first catch at sea / 海上把首批魚穫分類

Currently, it is best time for fishing. From January to September, it is good fishing season for trawler or "light circling". For "light" fishing, they won't go beyond ten nautical miles (18km) from shore. Some go as far as Qinglan port, Wen Chang or even Qi Zhou Yang (Seven Islands Ocean). Trawlers would go twice as far to twenty nautical miles. Since 1979 boats refrained from going to Xi Sha (Paracel Islands) fishing ground as it is more dangerous and fish prices sold there are at lower price. In the past, they would fish there for three months of the year and turned over their catch to the local Xi Sha fishing industry company. From New Year on, weather turns nice and can work until end of the Fourth or Fifth Moon on the lunar calendar. Boat trip around 160 nautical miles requiring over twenty hours at seven nautical miles per hour. After the Fourth Moon, south prevailing wind starts blowing at Hainan and wind becomes stronger.

Have never heard of pirates nor been harassed by one. Whereas they have run into other fishing boats from Hong Kong and Taiwan. When typhoon hit or engine trouble, those boats often dock here. They do not fish in Hong Kong waters as the distance is too far and time taken too long. But there are many Hong Kong boats arriving in recent years. There are some near-coast natural protected areas which prohibits shrimp catch from outside boats. The China Fishery Administration has set up to protect resources of the ocean.

His family has six in the household. Between 1980 to 1983, each production personnel can earn over Rmb100 in monthly income. Before 1980, each may make between 40-50 Yuan. Before 1979, his brigade only sold their catch to the government, never selling on their own. Since 1979, they are allowed to sell "high-price fish" with 30 to 40% of their catch. This practice allows for higher profit.

With more money in return, the initiative is much higher, so everyone rushes back to the sea and casts net. Those higher paid sales may yield two hundred Yuan per month. Each year a person may have over a thousand, and some may have over three thousand Yuan. Average may be around one to two thousand. Each production labor hand works for nine months.

Trawler catches "Gang Xian Yu" (Melon Coat Fish), locally called "Hong Xian Yu". What is scientifically called "Dao Li Yu" we call "Hong San Yu" (Golden Threadfin Bream). Catching "Ma Gao" (Mackerel) use "Lao Xian" net or hook. Now after New Year is the best fishing season until a month after Chinese New Year.

Each day out at sea pulling a net usually yields ten to twenty dan (100 catty or 50 kilo). Occasionally there may be twenty to thirty dan. Each trip out over twenty nautical miles can return with three thousand catty. There is no use of sonar fish-finder as it can only search the top and middle depth whereas deeper depth cannot be reached. Most nets reach the sea bottom with a fifty meter net width, going to a hundred meters depth. Each net weighs about three hundred catty. Each cable pulls over a hundred catty. Lighting boat usually only has eight horsepower and weighs 180 catty. Single trawler has two side boards, with sixty meter water depth. If deeper, the power is not enough to pull.

Trawler starts to let down net at 6am and raises it at around 11 to 12 noon. Each day fish twice before returning to port. If running into good catch, may set net three times. Fishing was handed down from ancestors, so even if given land he would not know how to farm.

Occasionally would run into fishing boats from Vietnam. Between 1981 and 1982 fishing boats are mainly

Drying cuttlefish and squid / 生曬花枝與魷魚
Second catch of day / 一天內第二批魚穫

filled with refugees. By 1983 they are rare. They can catch the flying fish and it tastes very fresh. Near Wen Chang there are plenty and their people love it. Here in the south, not so popular. Whenever running into a refugee boat, they often try to come to our side to ask for rice, oil or fish. From 1979, 1980 and 1981, seeing how pitiful they are we often allow them to come close. But later, there are cases of robbing the boat and people, plus beatings, so everyone refrained from letting them get close. Their boats are small, overcrowded with passengers and too small to reach Hong Kong, so they would try to take over our bigger boats to sail further. Besides among refugees there are complicated people too.

The brigade was changed to Xiang (village), and our Yu Gang Village has around 1,100 people, with five to six hundred households. In 1983, we caught a whale of over ten thousand kilo and over ten meters long. It was killed by fishing with dynamite. The commune West brigade pulled it back and it took two days. The government fishing company did not know how to deal with it and did not buy it. Later it was sold to an individual for over 300 Yuan to make oil.

In the past, some foreigners said they have seen our boats using dynamite to fish along the coast. This is because when the policy was relaxed, some fisherman using lights to fish started using dynamite as well, as the yield would be higher. One boat using dynamite would affect other's yield, so it forced others to follow and use the same. The Fishing Administrators cannot seriously control the situation, as such activities are difficult to monitor.

Fishing people usually do not sell fish at market. It generally passes through two hands before reaching market. Today at market, the big paired prawns are sold at four Yuan per half kilo, whereas the fisherman would sell at half that or less to the middleman. Squid is sold at seven to eight Yuan per half catty. But by the time it reaches market, it costs around 13 to 14 Yuan per half kilo. Cuttlefish is slightly over four Yuan per half kilo, and twice that at market.

When it was still under the commune system, all bigger boats had wireless radio for communications. It is for convenience, so when one boat runs into fish school can inform other boats of its whereabout. Today since the boats are privately owned and operated, no one likes to share such information. The government also took back the radios - over ten sets.

The fishery bureau would only purchase 8% of the catch. Two trawlers working together - each has an engine of 250 horsepower. Together they have 500 horsepower. Each boat is around 100 tons, and originally they

Sorted fish at bay / 已分類的漁獲抵達碼頭

Working with baby / 背著孩童工作

were part of the navy fleet, but retired. Each boat can carry over ten tons, and in one haul can bring in over two thousand dan of fish. Without ice to keep the catch, they cannot stay out at sea for long. If they stay too long, they would need to add salt to keep the catch from spoiling.

Sanya has hundreds of fishing boats. This is South Sea (Nanhai) Fishery District Unit. The other is Gang Xi (Harbor West) Fishery District Unit. Together they have eight fishing brigades. There are also four fishing brigades belonging to farming districts. Ai Xian County (Sanya) has thirteen brigades. Sanya harbor was opened to foreign boats since last year. After a typhoon it is the most busy. During 1983 typhoon season it received over fifty fishing boats from Taiwan, largest number ever. Since 1981 Marshall Ye Chien-Ying's announcement to Taiwan compatriots, they started arriving during typhoon season for shelter. Hong Kong boats have always come regularly. Nanhai district has over 7000 in population. Today we are visiting Yu Gang Village, which is in fact the former Yu Gang Brigade.

Fishing junk using sails can also net over ten thousand catty in one catch, meaning over a hundred dan. Starting with the lunar calendar ninth moon to following year second moon there is monsoon wind near Ai Xian county. So they fish here. By third moon they move to Le Dong, and in *fifth moon to Xiong Hai, Wen Cheng and Bei Ye area to work. By the ninth moon they return again to Sanya as the northeasterly wind picks up. Third moon the southwesterly wind prevails, whereas by fifth moon, fish near Xiong Hai. Motorized boats always hope the weather will be nice and calm, whereas sailing junks require wind to operate. Without wind, they cannot move.*

If boats go to Qi Zhou Yang (Seven Island Ocean), it is further and requires one to two days to return. If running into typhoon or windless days or headwind, then cannot come back even when a typhoon hits. Such danger happens from time to time. Now using double trawlers is much safer. Even when there are breakdowns, they won't happen both at the same time.

These days the Huanghua and Beifan fish all disappeared. Before there were plenty to be seen as long as the boats were out at sea. Motorized boats, day in day out, dredging the ocean, so everything is about all gone. The government must arbitrate and start fish cultivation.

Like this boat with 250 horsepower - if we had that in the old days in the 1950s, we would not bother to pull the net without at least ten thousand catty. Today, if you have four to five thousand catty, it is a great catch already. With five thousand catty, you can live quite well already. In the past when going to the Xi Sha (Paracel), even using line fishing can yield over a thousand catty a day. In 1959, while at Paracel Islands four persons in a small boat in just one night yielded two to three thousand catty. Now, no more.

When casting line, the fish follow the bait all the way to the surface. The furthest point reached was Zhong Yuan. In 1959, we reached also Vietnam's northern bay. During the Paracel typhoon in 1974, 108 fishermen died. At that time, when we got a shark, inside it had human body parts. Tried to sell the shark as fertilizer and still no taker.

Each time out at sea requires around 1,000 Yuan for diesel fuel. Government price is over 500 per ton. It started at just over 200 and then went up to 370, and occasionally up to 1200. Nonetheless you have to buy it at whatever price. One refills after slightly over half a month.

I started off at 8:30pm waiting at shore until 11pm when a small sampan took me to the boat. The boat went out at 3am. My driver Ah Hai and I slept on the upper deck above chief Ye Zhenxin of Yu Village. The owner-captain is Chen Yalou (47) and boat Number Ai Xian 11117. Woke up at 5:30am to observe from the front deck to see the dropping of the net.

The iron chain holding the huge net is very loud when released. The sky is barely paling. Boat continued sailing south. As they first released the net, firecrackers were let off for good fortune. A rope was sent to the accompanying boat to tie the other side of the net. Each boat maintained about a distance of 100 meters as they moved forward. Women on deck began cooking breakfast, or the morning meal. Ai Hai started getting seasick and vomited. Whatever went in came back out. By afternoon, he vomited over a dozen times. I joined him, but only three times. Each time I tried to stabilize myself while taking pictures or video, it got me dizzy and sick.

The boat has five to six families working jointly on board. The harvest will be divided based on labor heads on hand. A pair of boats operating together can yield over 200,000 Yuan each year. Each person can then receive a few thousand Yuan. The payout is also based on expertise rendered. The Captain and the skilled hands would each receive at least over three thousand.

At noon, the net was pulled up for the first time. It yielded around eight hundred catty. There are several major groupings of the catch, cuttlefish and squid were the most valuable. Once the catch was dumped on deck, they released the net again. Right away, everyone got busy separating the different fish on the front deck. Cuttlefish and squid got the priority in preparation. The fish net when up was all black, as the jets of ink of the cuttle fish and squid sprayed it dark. Different fish are put into baskets.

At around 4:30 in the afternoon the net was pulled up again. This time around 1500 catty was caught. Two rounds yielded over 2000 catty. As we sailed back to port it was around 5:30 pm. Small boats gathered around our boat to unload the catch. Each small boat would buy up entire baskets, be they good or bad. The highest priced cuttle fish and squid are not sold and stayed on boat. Once on shore, these boats' loads would change hands right away again to fish mongers who in turn would take them to market.

My rental car did not show up so we waved down a motorcycle and returned to my hotel at Lu Hui Tao (Deer Turning Head). Missed dinner by then, and made instant noodles in the room as dinner.

[There were no private restaurants back then and hotels only served within set hours, usually for one hour and early. The following day was January 13, a Friday, and I began my visit to the Yang Nan Islamic village and its mosque near Sanya. That was a precursor to my fourth National Geographic Expedition, later in 1984, to study the Islamic Frontiers and Silk Road... another story.]

附近的市場上，每半公斤烏賊人民幣一點三元，大對蝦半公斤秤起來約有八至十尾，要價四元；而海蜇則半公斤零點七元；檳榔果一百顆的價格是五元。

漁村村長葉鎮新，今年四十七歲，住在一棟屋齡三年的兩層樓房子，周邊許多未完工的房子與空屋。葉村長解釋，一開始政策上允許大家蓋新屋，於是人人開始興建，但忽然又有新政令，宣佈漁夫可以自購船隻，這下大夥兒趕緊停下蓋一半的房屋工程，打造新屋的錢轉向打造新船，因為船是生財工具，賺錢得靠它。葉村長是所謂的蜑家人，說的是粵語，葉家世世代代以來都定居於海南島，若要追溯起他們的祖籍源自中國何處，恐怕已不可考。村長夫妻一家八口，育有五個孩子與一孫。其中兩兒當漁夫，另一孩子任職高中老師，還有一個孩子在就學。葉村長口述道：

拖網漁船向來都兩艘一起出海。每艘船至少有十二至十五位船員。過去個人不能擁有自家漁船，漁船屬漁業公社所有，在公有系統運作下，船員編制的人數比現在還多。政策改變後，在個人營收分配的利益考量下，為節省人力成本，雖然每艘船人手比過去少，但工作效能卻提升不少，利潤當然也水漲船高了。這些船使用燈光圍捕，而漁船圍捕也需要更多人員投入，一般是十八人。小船圍網的動能，來自二十至四十匹馬力的引擎。目前，當地已不見有人用帆船捕魚，你所看見的那些帆船，大多來自外地。大部分漁船為當地船廠自行製造，少部分產自廣東沿海一帶的陽江。一些來自外地的帆船被當成貨船使用，而船上的帆則由海口市製造。

今天，幾乎百分百的船隻都屬私人用船。但在一九八三年之前，這些船隻都還屬於當地漁業大隊所有。隔年，這些船隻的價格開始大跌，一些成員多的大家庭開始買得起

船，小家庭則聯手出資合買船。每一艘船規模大約七至八噸重，有些稍大的重達十噸。從一九八二年開始，由於決策權開始鬆綁，委由更多地方區域主導，眼見商機不可失，交通大隊轉而投入製造小型船隻。這些船隻的引擎動能從十二至二十匹馬力不等，其中一台十二匹馬力的船要價七千元左右。一手交船，一手付錢，銀貨兩訖；資金若不足，可向銀行貸款。這裡大部分家庭高度仰賴船隻。但更早之前，從一九八〇年開始，每一戶人家獲政府分配一間房子，有些大家庭很幸運，分配到不只一間房子。

每逢農曆新年與特殊節日，所有漂流在外的船隻都回到港口，另外或遇八月至十月的颱風季，船隻也不出海。現在，正是出海捕魚的最佳時機。從一月至九月，是拖網捕魚或燈光圍捕的好時季，而燈光圍捕的範圍，則原會離岸逾十海浬之外。但也有些漁民會到清瀾港、文昌甚至遠赴七洲洋一帶的海域。拖網漁民最遠可以航行二十海浬之遙。打從一九七九年開始，政府禁止漁船進入西沙群島附近海域，除了因為海域凶險，當地的魚價也相對低得多。過去，他們一年會到西沙捕魚三個月，然後，再將漁獲直接賣到西沙當地的漁業工廠。不過，從新的一年開始，風調雨順，天候一路從年

Fish venders in market / 市場的魚販

Market venders / 市場攤販

Coral sold in street / 街上售賣的珊瑚

初好到農曆四、五月。一趟一百六十海浬的出海行程，至少得以每小時七海浬的速度前進，前後歷時二十個小時才能抵達目的地。農曆四月以後，海南島盛行吹南風，風勢一天比一天強。

他們從未聽過海盜，也沒有被騷擾等狀況，不過，他們卻曾在海上偶遇其他來自香港與台灣的漁船；每每颱風襲擊或引擎故障時，這些外來漁船經常得停泊此區港口。這群海南島漁民不會貿然到香港周遭海域捕魚，那距離對他們而言太遙遠，過於耗時費力。但近幾年倒是常見許多香港漁船頻繁出入此區，只是，中國漁業局已設定一些海洋資源的保育措施，鄰近沿海的一些保護區，已嚴禁外來漁船來此捕蝦。

葉村長一戶有六名成員。在一九八〇年至八三年之間，具備生產力的個人，每月收入為人民幣一百元。一九八〇年以前，個人月收入大約是四十至五十元。一九七九年以前，當地漁業公社只把他們的漁獲賣給政府，他們從未有機會自行處理買賣交易。一九七九年以後，他們才准予自售「高價位魚」，但僅限漁獲量的百分之三十至四十。即便只是有限度的開放自售，但對他們的營收仍是利多。收入增加了，產能與積極性也隨之提升，激勵更多人投奔大海，下網打魚。順利的話，每一個月最高可以攢得兩百元收入。推算下來，個人年收入可以累積超過一千元，運氣更好的話，一年可以賺到三千元；所以，平均一年一、兩千元是可預期的目標，扣除無法出海的時間，一年內的人力勞作時間是九個月。

拖網漁夫捕抓的「瓜衫魚」，當地人稱之為「紅線魚」；而我們一般所謂的「紅衫魚」（金線鯛魚），在生物學的正式稱謂其實是「刀鯉魚」；而捕撈「鯖魚」則得使用「撈線網」

或魚鉤。而最理想的捕魚季，從新的一年開始算起，一直延續到農曆年隔月。

每一天近海小船出海的漁獲量，一般大約收十至二十擔；偶爾一天內還可以有二、三十的漁獲量。每一趟超過二十海浬的打漁作業，一般可以滿載一千五百公斤而歸。他們不使用聲波定位的魚群探測儀，因為這類器具的識別範圍有限，一般從水面至海的中間層，無法探測至海底深處。拖網一般寬約五十公尺，重達一百五十公斤，可以深入一百公尺的海床底層展開捕魚作業；每一個纜繩的拉力至少超過五十公斤。燈光圍網的漁船一般的重量是九十公斤，動力輸出只有八匹馬力。單一拖網漁船左右兩側的側板寬深，可達六十公尺；若再深一些，則恐不足馬力把漁網拖拉起來。

清晨六點，開始把拖網放入海底深處，直到中午十一、十二點，再把網子拉起來。如此下網拉網，一日兩回。如果魚群多，或許還會下網三次。在這裡，捕魚是祖傳的家族事業，就算你給子孫留下一塊地，他們或許也不曉得如何拿起鋤頭農耕呢。

出海捕魚時，偶爾會遇見來自越南的漁船。一九八一至八二年那段期間，大部分越南漁船上都載滿難民。一九八三以後，難民現象才比較少見。難民會捕飛魚，尤其靠近文昌附近的海域，飛魚較多；其味鮮美，難民很喜歡。但在南方這一帶，飛魚則比較不普遍。每一次當這群漁夫與難民船擦肩而過時，對方會嘗試把船趨近，跟漁民要一些米、油或魚。回頭想，從一九七九年、一九八〇至八一年間，每每看見難民船便心生同情，經常讓他們靠過來。但後來聽聞一些好心助人反被連人帶船遭洗劫的案例，甚至還被毒打一頓，從此，漁船上人人自危，大家不再讓難民船靠近。一般而言，這些難民船不大，船上超載，人滿為患，小得無法航進香港，所以可想而知，他們需要奪下漁民的大船，才能航行得更遠。其實，船上除了難民外，還有其他來歷不明的閒雜人。

Small catch / 小魚穫
Sorting second catch / 為第二批魚穫分類

漁業公社已轉由各鄉主導，而我們的漁港村大約一千一百居民中，家庭戶數佔五、六百。一九八三年，漁民曾以炸藥捕魚法捕獲一條重量超過一萬公斤、長度逾十公尺的鯨魚。西部的漁業公社足足耗時兩天才把鯨魚拖回港。公社的漁業公司毫無頭緒，不知如何處理，也不願買下這隻大魚。後來，這隻鯨魚以三百元被賣給個體戶製油。

過去，有些外國人指稱看過他們的漁船在沿海一帶使用炸藥捕魚；背後緣由，其來有自：政策鬆綁後，為了提高收穫，原來使用燈光圍網的漁民也同時把炸藥派上用場。但問題是，使用炸藥捕魚法將影響其他漁船的捕魚作業與漁獲，因此，其他漁民不得不比照處理。雖然違法，但因這類活動難以監控，所以中國漁業局也無法完全掌控或從嚴查辦。

這裡的漁民一般不在市場上自行販賣漁獲，通常要經過兩次轉手，才送達市場。今天的市場上，大隻對蝦半公斤的價格是四元，但漁民賣給中盤商的價格只需市價的一半或更低；以魷魚來說，中盤商以半公斤七至八元價格向漁民買下後，一轉手在市場上的叫賣價便提高至半公斤十三、十四元。烏賊的批發價是半公斤四元，一放到市場上的價格便是兩倍起跳。

政策改變前，在漁業公社的經營模式下，所有大船都配有無線通

Kid help sorting cuttlefish / 小孩幫忙分類花枝

訊以確保聯繫與方便彼此通風報信。尤其當一艘漁船發現大片魚群時，可以即時通知其他船隻，前來他們的所在位置提供支援。但今天，各家漁船屬個人私有、個人私營，沒有人會想要分享這樣的訊息。另外，政府也將總計大約十台無線通訊設備收回。

一般而言，漁業署只負責買下漁民百分之八的漁獲量。兩艘拖網漁船同進同出，合作無間——每一艘的引擎動力是兩百五十匹馬力，兩艘合起來便有五百匹馬力的動力輸出；而每一艘漁船大約一百噸重，這些漁船的前身是「退役」後的海軍船艦。每一艘漁船可以承重十噸，一趟出海可以承載超過十萬公斤的漁獲重量。漁船上沒有冷凍設備，所以他們的出海時間無法太長久。如果需要在海上漂流稍久些，他們需要在漁獲上加鹽，以確保新鮮。

三亞市有上千艘漁船。這裡是南海區漁業署，另一個則是港西區漁業署。兩署部合起來總計有八家漁業公家單位，另外還有四家漁業單位分屬農業區。三亞市的崖縣則有十三家漁業公社。自去年開始，三亞港開放，讓外來船隻入港。一直以來，每遇颱風季，海港也隨之進入忙碌高峰期。還記得一九八三年的颱風季，三亞港接受超過五十艘來自台灣的漁船入港避風，創下有史以來最多台灣船隻入港的記錄。自一九八一年中國統帥葉劍英宣佈對台政策並發表了《告台灣同胞書》之後，台灣船隻開始把這裡當成颱風季的避風港。香港船隻則一如以往般頻繁進出。南海區域的人口，總計超過七千；今天我們所訪視的漁港村，其實前身正是漁港公社。

另外，漁船揚帆捕魚，也可以一次下網就收穫逾五千公斤的量。從農曆九月開始，直到隔年二月，是崖縣一帶的季風期，所以他們選擇在此捕魚。農曆三月後，他們便轉

移陣地到樂東縣，五月時則到瓊海、文城、北野一帶工作。農曆九月前，吹起東北季風時，他們再度返回三亞。三月吹西南季風，五月以前便可航向瓊海捕魚。開著機動漁船捕魚，最希望風平浪靜，天候穩定，只有帆船捕魚才希望吹大風，以借風使力，否則帆船便寸步難移。

如果漁船開到七洲洋，那算是比較遠的出海行程，來回時間至少需要一、兩天。假若老天興風作浪、或遇颱風與逆風，則歸期就難確定了。類似的危急狀況不時發生，但現在的拖網漁船一出海便出雙入對，雙船拖網的方式安全多了；即便有任何故障或意外，至少不會兩艘同時發生，還可相互支援。

過去，漁船一出海，悠游水面的黃花魚與白飯魚，多得肉眼可辨，但這陣子已不見牠們蹤跡。機動漁船日復一日在海洋中搜尋打撈，想必這些魚群已所剩不多。所以，政府必須對此積極裁決，開始魚類復育計劃。

比方說，以這艘兩百五十匹馬力的漁船為例──如果這是發生在一九五〇年的舊時代，若非漁獲重量達五千公斤，漁民根本不會拖網上船；但今不如昔，只要達兩、三千公斤的漁獲量便是大有斬獲了。一般而言，只要有兩千五百公斤的成績，日子便可過得比較輕鬆。過去在西沙群島一帶，即使只用傳統繩釣法，一天也有超過五百公斤的漁獲。他們憶起一九五九那年，他們四人共乘一艘小船，在西沙群島打魚，才一晚便有一、兩千公斤的捕獲量，成效斐然。但這樣的輝煌戰績，如今已不復見。

拋下繩線後，魚群一路隨餌到水面上。漁民最遠曾到中遠一帶進行打漁作業。一九五九年，他們也曾遠赴越南北方峽灣附近捕魚。另外，一九七四年大夥兒到西沙群島時，還曾因強颱襲擊，而致一百零八位漁民罹難。當時漁民捕獲的一條鯊魚，經開膛破肚後竟發現內有人類殘肢；最後即便把鯊魚當肥料售出也找不到買家。

每一次出海，漁船柴油費大約一千元。政府公定的柴油價格是每噸五百元。最初是兩百元，然後再調漲至三百七十元，偶爾油價大漲時也曾飆到一千兩百元。但無論價格如何，你無從選擇，只能買單。

跟著漁船出海那晚，我八點半便已在岸邊守候，枯等至晚間十一點才等來一艘小舢舨把我送到漁船上。凌晨三點，漁船出發。我的司機阿海和我，在船艙上層休息，村長葉鎮新則睡在我們下方。漁船船主兼船長是四十七歲的陳有佬，船號為崖縣 11117。清晨五點半，摸黑起早，迫不及待守在前方甲板，等著看漁民下網。

鬆開鐵鏈固定的大型漁網時，發出震耳欲聾的巨響。天色將亮未亮，漁船往南方航行。漁民出海第一次鬆開漁網時，還要燃放鞭炮，期待好運臨到，滿載而歸。一條大繩被拋到另一艘隨行船，以便把漁網的另一邊綁緊。兩艘漁船以維持一百公尺的距離，同時前進。甲板上的婦女開始煮早餐。阿海開始暈船、嘔吐，所有吃進肚子的東西，都「翻江倒海」吐出來；到中午前，他吐了十幾次。我也不例外，昏了頭而吐三次。每一次當我舉起相機拍照或錄影時，都想努力保持平穩，但仍頭暈目眩，非常不適。

漁船上的工作人員由五、六個家庭組成，因此，每一次出海的營收也將按人力來分配。成雙出海的兩艘漁船通力合作，一年的盈利所得大約是二十萬元，因此，順利的話，每人可分得數千元左右。當然，酬勞分配還要按專業能力來分配，船長與熟練的資深老手至少可獲三千元以上。

中午時分，漁網第一次被拖上船。一網漁獲重約四百公斤，被分成好幾種主要類別，

其中最值錢的，要數烏賊與魷魚。將漁獲甩落甲板上，漁民再度下網打魚。大夥兒立即一擁而上，在船前甲板上忙著把漁獲分類。想當然爾，烏賊與魷魚得優先處理。漁網上方烏黑一片，那是烏賊與魷魚噴墨汁的傑作。其餘不同種類的魚分別被放置籃子裡。

午後約四點半，再度收網。這一次，滿網漁獲，重量幾達七百五十公斤，連續兩次的捕獲量，總計一千公斤左右。當我們一行人返回港口時，已是下午五點三十分。環繞我們身邊的其他小船，準備把當日漁獲從大船卸下。每一艘小船都要不挑好壞一整籃子一整籃子的買下漁獲，只有最高價的烏賊與魷魚，船主不賣，留在船上。一旦上岸，這些漁獲量將直接轉手交到魚販手中，最終再送至市場上販售。我的出租車沒有出現，我們只好攔下一台機車，返回我們下榻的鹿回頭飯店。回時已晚，錯過晚餐時間，隨意煮個即食麵，聊以裹腹。

後記：當時沒有獨立餐廳，旅社也只在某個特定時段營業供餐，一般大約僅開放一小時或更短，隨後便打烊休息。隔天是一月十三日，星期五，我開始啟程，走訪羊欄鎮的伊斯蘭村莊與靠近三亞的清真寺。那一趟旅程，為我第四次領導《國家地理雜誌》探險埋下伏筆──我後來於一九八四年開始投入「伊斯蘭邊境與絲綢之路」的研究工作……不過，那又是另一回事了。

Fishing junk & trawler / 漁船與拖網漁船　　　　HM with Captain & Chief 1984 / HM 與船長和村長，攝於一九八四年

隔
離
時
刻

Q-TIME

Macau – April 20, 2021

Q-TIME
Notes on my two-week Quarantine

It was April 7 right after the Easter Holidays that I took the first bus out of Hong Kong Airport heading to Macau at 10:30 am. There were only three passengers on the bus, including my colleague Berry Sin. The day before, I had had my swab test at the Sanitorium Hospital, with results to indicate that I am not infected with Covid. After about an hour on the bus, we arrived at Macau's border immigration building.

Here at the building, entirely empty with exception of a few workers, I filled out some forms and scanned a QR code, which showed that I entered Macau as someone "Red," or prohibited from moving around. An officer took our ID cards and, after about an hour wait, ushered us on to a waiting bus that took the three of us to a hospital up the hill. A policeman stood guard where we waited, in case we were to run off into the open street. There we waited another hour for another swab test, before boarding the same waiting bus to be shuttled to the Lisboeta Hotel at Cotai, a brand new casino development of Macau.

This was one of the better quarantine hotels in Macau, and through a friend's connection, we were

HM at HK airport / HM 於香港機場　　　　　　　　　　　Hotel Room 913 / 酒店 913 號房間

given separate rooms on the high floor facing the nearby ocean, with a distant view of Lantau Island, a closer view of the Macau electric generating plant, and a direct view of the engineering infrastructure of the casino below us. I was almost oblivious to the bland gray-colored pipes, ducts and box-like structures, though it seemed to be a perfect maze for hide and seek.

I was thankful we faced east and would be able to see the sunrise if the spring fog and haze did not obliterate the far horizon. I was also thankful the room was spacious and came with both a shower and a tub and even a scale. I weighed myself upon arrival, as I would like to see how many kilos I gained in time. This would be my home for the next two weeks.

Soon a late lunch arrived with a ring at the door. The delivery was set on a high chair blocking my exit, as the "waiter" had long ago disappeared down the long hallway. The box meal was basic, even spartan, with some veggie and a few pieces of chicken with sauce and rice on the side. I wasted no time in calling Christina, the Macau secretary of Martin, one of our CERS directors.

Martin soon set up a "concierge" service to deliver whatever I wanted for the next two weeks. Delivery was only allowed each day from five to seven in the afternoon. My first order was rather sumptuous, including port, red & white wine, beer, cheese, sodas, chips, Korean instant noodles and kimchi, and an assortment of fruits. Corn flakes and milk were ordered as supplies for the following morning, as I knew soon I would stop altogether the hotel boxed delivery by the shadowy room service waiter.

Oh, yes... I also ordered from Christina an electric steamer to warm up my leftover food. As for fruits, I knew better than to order durian and sufficed myself with bananas, grapes and mangoes.

Structure above casino / 賭場外的建構物

By late afternoon, when my first order arrived, I felt the line-up of all the accessary niceties eased a little bit the impending pain and anxiety.

My first dinner catered from outside was a consolation prize, especially the fine wine Martin chose for me. I was looking forward to sipping my first glass of vintage Sandeman Port from 1980. Unfortunately, the cork was also of that vintage, and broke into the bottle as I tried delicately to open it with a Swiss knife corkscrew. A strainer would be called for in my next delivery. The Portuguese tart after supper was still a delight.

Several high-flying friends after viewing pictures I sent asked me how to have quarantine like mine. I gave three bits of advice. 1) get Martin to be on your board, 2) get Martin to be on your board, and 3) get Martin to be on your board.

Time flies, we often say. It was willing to slow down for me. In fact, it stopped.

It was my second day inside the Lisboeta and I had just woken up from a deep sleep. I rolled over to check my watch sitting on my bedside table. It said 10 o'clock. I was a bit shocked, as how could I have slept only an hour when I went to bed at 9. It would mean a long night ahead to morning, not

Spartan meal box / 差強人意的便當
Provision & supplies / 支援物資與供應

to speak of the long days and two weeks I had to last through inside this room.

As I got up for my night call, I glanced at the desk and saw the hotel clock reading, 5:55. That seemed more accurate, as I also noticed that the sky outside was paling a little. Suddenly, I realized that my watch, an Omega Solar Impulse, had stopped. It only winds up with motion, and the watch has been sitting for a day and a half. Even had it been attached to my wrist, it probably would have stopped, as I had been more or less a couch potato since checking into my hotel room.

While I quarantined for two weeks, the newspapers were quarantined only for hours, going through a process of decontamination and sterilization before arriving at newsstands around 9 pm each evening. Given there is no more hydrofoil service, all cargo, newspapers included, were shipped by slow boat from Hong Kong to Macau.

Our dispatch of the latest newsletter hot off the press arrived in three days, by SF express delivery. I ordered my first newspaper delivered after one week, and after two deliveries, decided to stop, as none of the news seems all that relevant when you are in detention. Soon, I used the papers to reminisce on old days, folding them into paper boats or even a pistol to play with. I always tell myself to care first about things I can have an impact on, and, secondly, things that can impact me, immediately. Neither seemed to be relevant at the moment. I never watch TV, and remained true to that even stuck to my room for two weeks.

As I had limited space and weight in my luggage, which I must carry into China myself after quarantine, I knew I could either read a book or write a book. I opted for writing, and did not even bring one book to read. Fortunately, that decision seemed a sound one, as I finished the last four chapters of my next book in no time at all.

A week into my quarantine, on April 14, corresponding to the 13th in the US, I made a call to San Francisco, despite the roaming charges on my Hong Kong phone. It was to Moon Chin, my pilot friend, on his 108th birthday. We chatted merrily just as he was ready for his birthday cake. His relatives asked for me to lead off with a birthday song. After that, I felt much better about my current status of confinement. After all, Moon, at such a senior age, had been confined to his home for the last couple of years, even before the pandemic.

As time went on, I finally learned to use Tao Bao for the first time on my iPad and browsed through the many inflatable kayaks on display. I finally decided on two to order for our upcoming expedition. That's not a small accomplishment, as I had heard about this addictive virtual shopping mall for several years.

Very quickly I also found out more not only about my room, but also about myself. Now to "Q-time,", or kill time, I take two baths a day. When the

Moon at 108 / 陳文寬一百零八歲生日

indoor temperature is set right, there seems no need to wear any clothes, at best wearing my bath robe. Thus, no laundry is ever needed. I brought my pipe, not so much to puff as to think while looking at the smoke, in case I am seriously bored. But that never happened, and I only took one puff and left it aside. Likewise, my near-sighted glasses were left at the window for two weeks without my touching them at all.

Once a week had passed and the midway point was reached, a count down began. As if winter had arrived, the days became shorter and shorter. Likewise my supply of fine wine. At the end of one week, the wine was gone. Fresh supply of red and white, even better than the first batch, was delivered again, courtesy of Martin. Aware of the maxim "there's no free lunch," I continued ordering only dinner, but twice the portion so I could save half for the following day's lunch, warmed up in the steamer.

As another proverb goes, "no pain no gain," but I did not feel any pain during the two weeks. Surely I did not pay the huge price some others did in heading to special retreat enclaves for meditation to nurse their body and soul. So despite eating well and having no exercise, I gained no weight. Instead, I actually lost almost a kilo at the end of two weeks. There goes all the theory on weight gain and loss, diet or not. Maybe I should not only gauge my weight, but measure whether my neck is getting longer by the day, as I gained anxiety and anticipated the coming of liberation day.

I did however find out more about myself. I am known among my friends and relatives for being a Coke addict. I've never bothered to counter that notion. On the first day of my checking in on April 7, my delivery included six bottles of Coke. Not one was open as of the 16th. I finally opened my first bottle of Coke on the 11th day, to go down with my Portuguese tart dessert after dinner. I really didn't care all that much about Coke. Of the Cream Soda, only one was consumed, over a period of four days.

My mind on the other hand has started wandering, at times into a distant world that is more and more irrelevant to my immediate existence. I think of human kind descending into an abyss such that the only way to describe the world we are in is either cynically or sarcastically. My former approach of being philosophical is gradually being marginalized.

Maybe I am also gradually spacing out, into the celestial realm. Suddenly I recall an astronaut I had met at a dinner in Hong Kong. Buzz Aldrin was a member of the Apollo 11 Mission. In July 1969, a month before I

Japanese meal delivered / 外送日式午餐

My Porto photo & vintage Port / 我的波爾圖照片與陳年砵酒

arrived in the U.S. for college, he piloted the lunar landing module "Eagle" onto the surface of the moon.

Neil Armstrong left the module and became the first man on the moon - Buzz would follow a few minutes later, becoming the second. Within moments, he took that famous picture of the footprint in the fine dust on the surface of the moon.

Upon re-entering earth from space and "landing" in the ocean, they were picked up by the aircraft carrier Hornet and quickly rushed into quarantine for fear of contamination after exposure to extraterrestrial material. That tiny capsule for their quarantine was certainly smaller than the hotel room I was in right now. It was converted from an Airstream camper trailer.

Their time of quarantine, despite being national and worldwide heroes, was 21 days. On top of that, the entire mission in space was an additional eight days, with three astronauts crammed into the Command Module, ten feet tall and twelve feet wide at the base, roughly the size of a large car. Now my time in quarantine has been only 14 days. Suddenly, I felt quite privileged.

Tomorrow I will reach the end of my journey, after two weeks of Q-time. Stepping out of my room will be a small step for mankind, if at all, but a giant leap for me.

Apollo Command Module / 阿波羅指揮艙
Underdeck USS Hornet / 大黃蜂號航空母艦下層甲板

隔離時刻

檢疫隔離兩週筆記

復活節假期一結束，四月七日當天，上午十點三十分，我搭乘第一班巴士離開香港機場，直奔澳門。巴士上只有三名乘客，包括我的同事冼小姐。前一天，我才在香港養和醫院接受篩檢，取得新冠肺炎的陰性報告，確定無感染。一小時車程後，我們抵達澳門邊界的出入境大樓。

大樓裡除了幾位工作人員外，門可羅雀，不見任何旅客。我填好表格，完成掃描，我被標示為「紅字號」人物，以此身份入境澳門，換句話說，我被禁足，與世隔絕。一位官員把我們的身份證收走，枯等一小時後，我們被帶上一台守候已久的巴士上，巴士把我們三人載送到山坡上的一家醫院。抵達目的地後，再等一小時接受篩檢，身邊一名員警全程監護「陪等」，唯恐我們逃到街上。結束後，我們再被原巴士載到路氹的澳門葡京人飯店，一座澳門新發展的賭場建設。

這是澳門其中一間風評不錯的隔離飯店，透過朋友的協助，我們很幸運被分配到近頂樓面海每人一間的單人房，窗外景致，盡收眼底——遠眺大嶼山，近一點是澳門發電廠，往下俯瞰則是賭場的工程建設；我對那些暗淡的灰色煙囪、管子與箱型結構一無所知，看起來像極了完美的迷宮，適合捉迷藏。

我們的房間坐西朝東，假若春天濃霧與陰霾沒有把遠方的地平線遮蔽，日出美景可以一覽無遺，這真令我心懷感謝。還有一個值得慶幸的，是房內空間寬敞，浴室還配置了淋浴間與浴缸，甚至連浴室磅秤都備齊了。我站上體重計自我量測一下，隨時掌握這段「以飯店為家」的兩週內，到底會增加多少體重。

不久，門鈴響起，午餐送上門。一開門，只見一張高腳椅擋住出入口，餐點就放在椅子上；探頭望向長長的走道，早已不見「服務生」蹤跡。餐點菜色差強人意，一些青菜與幾片雞肉伴醬，一旁是白飯。我當機立斷，隨即致電中國探險學會其中一名董事馬丁的澳門秘書，克莉絲丁娜。

馬丁立即安排了「門房」服務，負責打點我未來兩週提出的所有需求；遞送時間僅限每日下午五點至七點。我的首批訂餐要求稍微奢華些，品項包括砵酒、紅白酒、啤酒、乳酪、汽水、薯片、韓國泡麵與泡菜，還有各種水果。另外額外加點的玉米片與鮮奶，是為隔天早餐多準備的補給品，因為我知道自己很快便將終止那位「魅影」般的服務人員所提供的便當送餐服務。

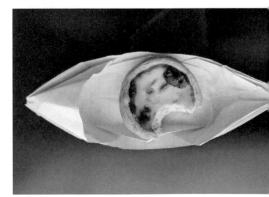

Breakfast cereal / 早餐麥片
Coke with Po tart / 可樂與葡式蛋撻

Fine wine / 美酒

哦，對了⋯⋯我還向克莉絲丁娜要了一台電子蒸鍋，可以隨時把吃不完的食物蒸熱。至於水果，我不致於糊塗到要求榴蓮，只要給我香蕉、葡萄與芒果，便滿足矣。午後，我的第一批貨送達，眼前令人食指大動的各式美食，如願以償，稍稍紓解了我即將坐困愁城的痛苦與焦慮。

我的第一頓外送晚餐，真是我的安慰獎，尤其是馬丁為我精挑細選的好酒。我滿心期待要淺酌一口一九八〇年釀造的聖地門陳年砵酒。只不過，軟木塞也很陳年，正當我以瑞士刀的開瓶器小心翼翼地嘗試開瓶時，軟木塞竟碎裂在酒瓶裡，真令我「飲恨」。下一批點貨項目內，得趕緊把過濾器含括在內。無論如何，餐後的葡式蛋撻仍讓我心滿意足。

我把這些照片上傳到社群媒體上，一些「有為者亦若是」的朋友紛紛探詢，要如何才能享有我這般禮遇式的隔離生活。我大方提供三大秘訣：第一，讓馬丁成為你的董事一員。第二，讓馬丁成為你的董事一員。第三，讓馬丁成為你的董事一員。

時光飛逝啊——我們總是這麼感歎。但這回，時光樂於為我停留。事實上，它真的停滯不動呢。

這是我待在澳門葡京人飯店的第二天，剛從一頓深眠中醒來。我

轉身查看床櫃上的手錶。手錶指向十點整。我有些吃驚，明明九點上床，怎麼可能我才睡一小時便起床？那意味著我還得熬過漫漫長夜才能到隔天清晨，更別提還有無盡的長日與未來兩個禮拜的時間，我都得在這斗室裡咬牙苦撐。

摸黑起床後，我瞥一眼桌上的飯店時鐘，咦，是五點五十五分。這看來準確又合理多了，我也發現窗外天空開始有些微弱的光線。我赫然驚覺，原來我的歐米茄行動驅動腕錶徹底停工了，這機械錶是靠手腕活動上發條，但它已靜止不動超過一天半了；就算手錶套在我的手腕上，它仍舊可能停滯，因為我從踏入飯店那一刻至今，基本上已差不多成了「沙發薯仔」——足不出戶，窩在沙發吃薯片的宅男。

當我被隔離兩週時，報紙則只被隔離數小時，歷經一段除汙與消毒程序，再於每晚九點送到售報處。現在水翼船停航，所有貨運，包括報紙只能由慢船從香港運送至澳門，難免阻延。

Vietnamese meal / 越南菜午餐　　　　Shanghainese meal / 上海菜午餐　　　　Seafood meal / 海鮮午餐

Buzz Aldrin with CERS friends /
伯茲・艾德林與中國探險學會之友

學會最新一期的會員通訊，由順豐快遞在三天內從香港送達。而我訂閱的第一份報紙則在一週後才收到，飯店送了兩次報，我便決定喊停，因為當你形同軟禁時，所謂新聞，其實也沒什麼意義了。不久，這些報紙竟讓我「睹物思情」而懷舊起來，我開始摺紙船或甚至摺成手槍來把玩。我經常告訴自己，首先應該關注我能影響的事，其次再留意那些會立即影響我的事。只是，這兩件事在當下那樣的時刻，差異似乎不大；唯一能落實的，是這段足不出戶的兩週，我完全沒有看電視——這我倒是做到了。

我能攜帶的行李空間與重量都有限，考量隔離兩週後我便得啟程前往中國，所以我局限自己只能二選一：讀一本書或寫一本書。我選擇書寫，所以連一本書都沒帶。我慶幸自己選對了，我幾乎分秒不浪費，一口氣把我下一本書的最後四章都完成了。

隔離滿一週，四月十四日當天剛好是美國那一邊的十三日，雖然使用我的香港電話打國際漫遊所費不貲，但我還是撥了通電話到舊金山給我的飛機師老朋友陳文寬，慶賀他的一百零八歲生日。我們相談甚歡，他那一邊的生日蛋糕也已準備上場了。陳文寬先生的親人在電話那一頭起哄，要我帶大家一起唱「生日歌」。掛上電話後，我想起如此高齡的文寬，在過去幾年，甚至早在疫情之前，便已足不出戶，居家照護。當下，我對自己這段閉門禁足的狀態，頓覺沒那麼糟糕了。

時間慢速移動，我終於在平板電腦上生平首次學會使用淘寶，瀏覽了各種展示的充氣獨木舟，最後決定為接下來的探險訂購兩隻。完成購物後的成就感，使我想起幾年前曾聽人說過，這類虛擬購物商場會令人愛不釋手而網購成癮。

我很快便對這間房間有更多新發現，也更認識自己了。不管是為了「隔離時刻」，或為消磨時光，我一天洗兩次澡。一旦室內溫控設定好，其實，也無需穿衣服了，間中套上沐浴袍，連衣服換洗都省略了。我把煙斗帶在身邊，心想或許抽一口菸，呼出的縷縷輕煙可以紓解我極度苦悶的日子。但預期中的煩悶並未發生，而我自始至終只抽了一次，煙斗便被擱置一旁；一如我的近視眼鏡，一連兩週都被置於窗戶邊，連碰都沒碰。

一週過去了，這條隔離之路已走一半，倒數計時開始。就像冬天一到，白晝愈短，恰似我逐漸見底的好酒。最後那週，酒已飲盡。但設想周到的馬丁，立即再送來紅酒與白酒，品質甚至比第一批更香醇。我依舊只訂晚餐外送，但謹記「天下沒有免費的午餐」，於是我訂了雙份晚餐，把一份留至隔天中午，蒸熱了當午餐。

另有一句話說：「沒有付出努力，就沒有收穫」，不過，這兩週我倒沒受太多苦。當然我也不像其他人付上高昂代價參加特殊群體的退隱靜思體驗團，滋養身心靈。不過，雖然這段時間我吃得好且沒有任何運動，我的體重卻不增反降，兩週內少了一公斤。增肥或減重，進食或禁食，各派理論，眾說紛紜。或許我要量測的不是體重，而是我的脖子長度，這段期間日夜翹首「引領」，焦躁而殷切企盼我的自由日，恐怕脖子也因此伸長了。

回頭檢視，我確實有更深入的自我認識。我在朋友與親屬中是出了名的可樂成癮者。我從不想為此

爭辯或駁斥。打從四月七日第一天入住，我的第一批外送物品中就含括六瓶可樂。一直到十六日，前後十天內，所有可樂都原封不動。到第十一天，我終於打開第一瓶可樂，搭配我的葡式蛋撻，當晚餐的飯後甜點。可樂對我而言，其實真的可有可無；至於忌廉汽水，四天內我也只喝了一瓶。

與此同時，我的內心千頭萬緒，思緒飄蕩至遙遠的世界，與我當下的實體存在越來越疏離與隔絕。我想起人類陷落如此萬丈深淵，最終只能以事不關己或尖酸刻薄的方式，來解釋我們所置身的世界。我原來想以哲學思辨當出路，但這樣的解構也越來越薄弱與邊緣化。

或許，我自己也逐漸抽離而與世隔絕了吧。我忽然回想多年前，曾在香港與一位太空人共進晚餐。他是曾經參與人類首次登陸月球太空飛行任務「阿波羅十一號」的伯茲・艾德林 (Buzz Aldrin)。一九六九年七月，就在我抵達美國入大學升造的前一個月，他駕駛「鷹號」登月艙，著陸月球。

尼爾・阿姆斯壯 (Neil Armstrong) 首先離艙而成為人類歷史上首位登陸月球的人——幾分鐘後，伯茲也跟上，成為第二位登月者。就在那關鍵時刻，他拍了那張引起世人矚目的照片——人類足跡踏在細塵如粉末的月球表面上。

從太空返回地球並「濺落」大海時，三位太空人隨後由「大黃蜂號」航空母艦協助登上救生筏，並立即讓他們接受隔離，唯恐他們因曝露於地球以外而沾染不明的外星物質。我可以想像，當時那小小的彈丸隔離空間——由 Airstream 露營拖車改造——肯定

比我現在所置身的飯店房間，還要狹小得多。

即便以全球英雄之姿自外太空凱旋而歸，他們還是得接受長達二十一天的隔離。除此以外，還得加上八天在外太空時，三個太空人踡縮於十尺高、十二尺寬、體積約為一大台車的登月艙內。思及此，反觀我這十四天的隔離時間，頃刻間，頓覺自己何等萬幸而欣慰。

明天，我這趟為期兩週的隔離之旅將走到終點。踏出房門的這一步將是人類的一小步，但對我而言，肯定是我的一大步。

Airstream trailer on left & Apollo capsule on right aboard USS Hornet /
大黃蜂號航空母艦上，左為 Airstream 露營拖車，右為阿波羅登月艙

戀
戀
木
棉

ROMANCE WITH COTTON TREE

Macau – April 13, 2021

ROMANCE WITH COTTON TREE

The little boy was about five years old. He was living in an old two-story house below Bonham Road in the mid-levels of Hong Kong. At night, looking out from the balcony, his nanny would tell him that the flickering lights across the harbor were ghosts winking at him. He would pull up his blanket further to cover himself when going to bed.

Outside the house was a large terrace with a few trees. They seemed like giants as the young boy looked up to the clear blue sky. The branches reached out sideways like parallel limbs perpendicular to the trunk. It was before he knew what seasons meant, except for being dressed up or down as the temperature changed.

He remembered, however, picking up those very large red flowers, each somewhat bigger than his tiny hands. They usually dropped each year at the same time when his blue silk jacket was taken off of him as the temperature warmed. Once, one of these flowers dropped on his head and he cried, running back into the house to his mother's arms.

One day, he received a shot given by a doctor making a house call, and he again cried, but much

HM as a little boy / 小時候的 HM

louder, as the needle went into his butt. But he saw the elders only got theirs on their arms. Pills were wrapped inside paper and crushed into pieces before he was made to swallow the bitter powder. He, however, relished the sweet taste of a syrupy oil spoon-fed to him.

Just as his sweater was also taken off his body, perhaps a month after the flower dropped on his head, there started floating in the sky some white stuff. This too would drift to the ground. By this time, green leaves had started filling up the tree. His nanny would pick up some of the fluffy stuff and take it inside the house. There, she would open her pillow case and stuff it in to refill the pillow.

"This is the same stuff inside your silk-lined jacket," the nanny told the little boy. As the days went by, his shoe sizes grew from 1 to 2. The walk each day to his kindergarten, two blocks away behind an old church, seemed shorter and shorter. The boy grew, and small toys changed from wood to iron, and then, later still, to plastic.

As time flew by, what seemed a very long day, week, month, or even year became shorter, as the boy became a teenager, a young adult, middle aged, finally arriving at old age. His internal clock raced now, making time feel shorter as it became a smaller fraction of the time he had lived through.

But the red flowers continued to bloom year after year, and the cotton-like fluffy stuff continued to drift down from the sky. He now realized that it was the Cotton Tree, also known as kapok, that had so fascinated him since childhood. Once an important commodity cargo shipped across the ocean from Asia to Europe and America as stuffing for mattresses and cushions, it had long since been replaced by synthetic fiber.

Years went by, and he had long given up all his toys. However, every year he would continue to pick up the red flowers, putting them into pots or even as a floating plaything for his bath. And his pillow, stuffed with that white, fluffy stuff, cushioned his head as his hair grew from black to gray and then white.

Fortunately, the vaccination shots he once received in his butt as a child had long ago moved to his arm.

Long live the Cotton Tree, Amen.

戀戀木棉

當年，小男孩五歲，住在香港半山區般咸道一間雙層平房裡。夜幕低垂時，他從家中陽台往外眺望，小男孩的保姆告訴他，那些映照在海港上閃爍的燈火，是鬼魂向他眨眼示意，嚇得他牢牢地鑽進被窩，拉高棉被才能入睡。

屋外大平台上種了幾棵樹。每一次當他抬頭凝視清澈藍天時，這些樹仿若參天巨人般，高聳屹立。枝椏伸向路旁，像樹幹垂直開出的平行四肢。小男孩對四季還懵懂無知，唯一的認知是隨著溫度起伏，身上的衣服或多或少，或厚或薄，如此而已。

他依稀記得撿起那些大朵的紅花，每一朵都比他小小手掌心還要大。每一年，就在天氣漸暖、他開始脫下藍色絲棉襖時，這些紅花便同時凋謝，繁華落盡。有一次，一朵紅花不偏不倚落在他頭上，他驚慌而哭，趕緊跑回家，直撲母親懷裡。

有一天，醫生到家裡來為家人注射。醫生在小男孩臀部扎了一針，他又哭了，他這回哭得更聲嘶力竭。環顧四周，奇怪，大人那一針怎麼都打在手臂上。大人還會把藥丸先在紙裡壓碎成粉末，然後迫他吞下這些苦澀藥粉。不過，被餵到口裡甜甜的糖漿藥水，還是叫他回味。

也許就在「花落頭頂」事件後一個月左右，他開始脫下毛衣時。天空飄起白綿綿的東西，輕如羽毛飄落地上。差不多同一時節，樹上開始冒出嫩葉。小男孩的保姆會撿起這些毛絨棉絮帶回家裡；再把枕頭套解開，將撿回來的那些棉絮往枕頭內裡塞滿滿。

「這小玩意兒，和你絲棉襖襯裡的東西，是一樣的。」保姆告訴小男孩。日月如梭，小男孩的鞋碼從一號增至二號。他開始上幼稚園——就在老教堂後方兩條街之外——這段路，越走越短。小男孩長大了，他的小玩具材質也跟著轉變，從木頭到鋼鐵，再後來是塑膠。

歲月如流，原來感覺的漫漫長日、一週一月，甚至一年，轉瞬即逝，眨眼間，小男孩進入少年、青年、中年階段，最終步入暮年。他的生理內置時鐘開始爭分奪秒，時間越覺短促了，短得像他漫長人生中的其中一小部分。

年復一年，紅花持續盛開，毛絨般棉絮繼續從空中飄落。如今他已知曉，當年令小男孩目眩神移的棉絮紛飛，是木棉樹，也被稱為英雄樹。木棉曾經一度是大宗貨櫃船運的重要商品，從亞洲出口至歐洲與美國各地，用作床墊與椅墊的重要填充物。不過，合成纖維早已取而代之了。

年逾花甲，兒時的那些玩具，已不復存在。但每一年，他依舊採擷紅花，將之放盤中或當泡澡時漂浮水中的玩物。而塞滿他枕頭內裡的，仍是那些蓬鬆的白色棉絮，枕墊著他的頭；唯一改變的，是枕頭上的一頭黑髮，已然斑白。

慶幸的是，當年只能往臀部注射的疫苗，老早便已轉移陣地到手臂了。

木棉樹萬歲，阿們。

國家圖書館出版品預行編目 (CIP) 資料

齊物逍遙 . 2020-2021 = Enlightened Sojourn. 2020-2021 / 黃效文著 .
-- 初版 . -- 新北市 : 依揚想亮人文事業有限公司 , 2021.12
面 ; 公分　中英對照
ISBN 978-986-97108-8-6（精裝）
1. 旅遊文學 2. 世界地理

719　　　　　　　　　　　　　　　　　　　　110019661

齊
物
逍
遙 2020-2021

作者‧黃效文｜攝影‧黃效文｜發行人‧劉鋆｜美術編輯‧Rene｜責任編輯‧島民創意有限公司｜翻譯‧
童貴珊｜法律顧問‧達文西個資暨高科技法律事務所｜出版社‧依揚想亮人文事業有限公司｜經銷商‧
聯合發行股份有限公司｜地址‧新北市新店區寶橋路 235 巷 6 弄 6 號 2 樓｜電話‧02 2917 8022｜印刷‧
禹利電子分色有限公司｜初版一刷‧2021 年 12 月（精裝）｜ ISBN‧978-986-97108-8-6｜定價 1300 元｜
版權所有　翻印必究｜ Print in Taiwan